Ptsd

The Psychology of Post-traumatic Stress Disorder

(Compassionate Strategies to Begin Healing From Childhood Trauma)

Forrest Franco

Published By **Kate Sanders**

Forrest Franco

Ptsd: The Psychology of Post-traumatic Stress Disorder (Compassionate Strategies to Begin Healing From Childhood Trauma)

ISBN   978-0-9958508-5-9

Legal & Disclaimer

Table Of Contents

Chapter 1: Recognizing Ptsd Symptoms

Common Symptoms of PTSD

The signs and symptoms of PTSD can be severa and complex, with many people struggling to understand the underlying reason in their distress. Let's find out the commonplace signs and symptoms and signs of PTSD, dropping moderate on this difficult situation and empowering you, the reader, to take high-quality steps in overcoming it.

1. Re-experiencing the Trauma: One of the hallmark signs and symptoms and signs of PTSD is the extreme and involuntary reliving of the disturbing event. This can show up in severa techniques:

a) Flashbacks: Sudden, vivid memories that play out as despite the fact that the trauma goes on all all over again. Flashbacks can be brought approximately thru manner of factors of hobby, sounds, or smells that resemble components of the specific event.

b) Nightmares: Disturbing dreams related to the trauma that disrupt sleep and make contributions to fatigue.

c) Intrusive thoughts: Unwanted, distressing thoughts approximately the disturbing event that usually intervene into regular lifestyles.

2. Avoidance Behavior: Individuals with PTSD regularly try to avoid some component that could remind them in their disturbing experience:

a) Avoiding locations, events, or conditions that might in all likelihood purpose recollections of the trauma.

b) Evading conversations or interactions with others about the annoying occasion.

c) Suppression of mind and emotions associated with the trauma in an try to compartmentalize or forget approximately approximately the revel in without a doubt.

three. Emotional Numbing: PTSD patients may enjoy emotional numbness or detachment as a protection mechanism towards overwhelming emotions. This can involve:

a) Difficulty feeling first-rate feelings consisting of love and satisfaction.

b) Lack of interest in previously amusing sports.

c) A experience of emotional distance from buddies and circle of relatives individuals.

d) Struggles with intimacy and do not forget building in relationships.

4. Hyperarousal Symptoms: People dealing with PTSD may additionally moreover show heightened states of arousal or alertness, as their our bodies hold to answer to perceived

threats in their environment. This kingdom includes:

a) Insomnia: Difficulty falling or staying asleep, ensuing in chronic exhaustion.

b) Irritability: Increased feelings of anger and frustration, principal to emotional outbursts.

c) Hypervigilance: Constantly scanning surroundings for potential dangers, making it difficult to lighten up or pay interest.

d) Startle reaction: Overreacting to sudden noises or sudden modifications in environment, at the side of jumping at the sound of a slammed door or a dropped object.

e) Difficulty concentrating: Impaired cognitive characteristic, together with forgetfulness, disorganization, and intellectual confusion.

5. Physical Symptoms: The outcomes of PTSD are not confined to the mind. The sickness can also purpose physical manifestations:

a) Chronic pain: Persistent headaches, muscle aches, or joint pain unrelated to any precise harm.

b) Digestive issues: Sufferers may also revel in gastrointestinal problems together with irritable bowel syndrome (IBS) and ulcers.

c) Cardiovascular problems: PTSD can result in an prolonged risk of coronary coronary heart assault and stroke due to ongoing strain responses.

d) Weakened immune system: Increased vulnerability to infections and infection because of stress-brought on reductions in immunity.

6. Negative Thoughts and Beliefs: PTSD may additionally additionally precipitate horrible self-perceptions and ideals approximately the arena:

a) Self-blame: Believing that they may be at fault for the stressful event or could have avoided it in a few manner.

b) Pessimism: Persistent emotions of hopelessness and despair about the destiny.

c) Distrust: Viewing the area as an inherently volatile vicinity and believing that others can't be relied upon for help or expertise.

d) Shame and guilt: Internalizing feelings of disgrace and guilt regarding their evaluations, predominant to faded vanity and self-worth.

How PTSD Affects Daily Life

Living with put up-traumatic strain illness (PTSD) is a daily war for lots who've professional traumatic events. The lingering outcomes of trauma could make even the most previously mundane sports activities hard to navigate. Here are a few common demanding conditions confronted through manner of people with this circumstance:

1. Sleep disturbances: One of the maximum common struggles for those with PTSD are troubles with sleep. Individuals may experience normal nightmares or hassle falling asleep and staying asleep. As a result,

those sleep disturbances regularly result in daytime fatigue and reduced cognitive functioning, making it hard to stay targeted finally of the day.

2. Work or faculty troubles: Concentrating on tasks can be almost not possible at the same time as chronic thoughts and reminiscences of demanding occasions occupy one's thoughts. These disruptions can have an effect on humans with PTSD at every paintings or school, fundamental to progressed absenteeism and regular performance troubles. Frequent interest lapses not only effect productiveness but moreover contribute to feelings of incompetence and alienation from colleagues or classmates.

3. Relationship issues: Communication and connecting with others are important additives of healthful relationships. However, PTSD often creates barriers within the ones areas for affected individuals, as they'll isolate themselves from friends and family

contributors or display off remote or cold conduct. Trust issues also can stand up at the same time as someone with PTSD struggles to permit others in, ensuing in relational isolation that further exacerbates intellectual fitness annoying conditions.

4.   Self-damaging   conduct: Coping mechanisms play an crucial function in coping with emotional ache; but, for people residing with PTSD, they do not continuously gift themselves as beneficial techniques. Many human beings may want to probable flip to substance abuse or brilliant volatile behaviors as a way to numb their feelings or regain a experience of manage over their lives briefly. This self-unfavorable behavior can all at once spiral out of control, intensifying present issues in location of presenting remedy from them.

five. Mental health struggles: Living with PTSD commonly consists of grappling with one-of-a-kind highbrow fitness conditions, inclusive of melancholy or tension issues, growing a complex set of disturbing situations for the character trying to get better. These co-taking area troubles can also moreover regularly overshadow PTSD symptoms themselves and make contributions to a non-stop cycle of worsening highbrow fitness.

6. Physical health problems: PTSD isn't absolutely a intellectual health scenario; it has physical implications as well. Chronic pressure also can motive complications, stomachaches, or muscle pain in human beings with PTSD. Additionally, ongoing fatigue can weaken the immune device and result in not unusual illnesses.

7. Sensitivity to triggers: People with PTSD are often pretty liable to triggers—cues from their environment that remind them of the stressful event. A unique sound, fragrance, or photograph can initiate excessive emotional reactions, inflicting human beings with PTSD to end up increasingly more vigilant and fearful of their every day lives.

8. Emotional numbness: In an try and shield themselves from in addition emotional ache, human beings with PTSD should probably emerge as emotionally "numb," making it difficult for them to each enjoy and express emotions. This detachment can reason feelings of isolation and save you the formation of huge relationships.

9. Guilt and shame: Self-blame is a not unusual symptom of PTSD as humans may also query their movements or inactivity in the end of the demanding occasion, frequently vital to emotions of guilt or shame. This introspection may be overwhelming and may hinder improvement in recovery from trauma.

Identifying Triggers

Life is a series of occasions and interactions that allow us to test, expand, and thrive. Each revel in shapes our perspective, contributing to the right direction we look at. However, for people suffering from PTSD, high high-quality people, environments, and stimuli can motive terrific and debilitating recollections of past trauma. These triggers remind us that the road to overcoming PTSD isn't always linear, but instead marked by way of the usage of detours and bumps along the way. It becomes vital to come to be aware about the ones triggers in case you need to govern and ultimately conquer PTSD.

A motive is any event or stimulus that causes an individual with PTSD to re-experience trauma-associated mind, feelings, and physical sensations. Triggers can range extensively among people and can prevent end result from seemingly unrelated conditions. They may be tangible gadgets, particular situations, or sports that set off an character's internal war closer to their trauma.

The identification of these triggers performs a essential feature inside the restoration way through permitting people with PTSD to boom coping techniques for handling and warding off them on the identical time as critical. Recognizing one's triggers furthermore empowers individuals to regain manipulate over their lifestyles and make knowledgeable alternatives on their route in the route of recuperation.

Types of Triggers

1. Environmental Triggers: The environment or contexts that remind an man or woman of their worrying event may additionally additionally elicit a reaction. Examples consist of crowded places, dark rooms, or specific sounds or smells associated with the trauma.

2. Emotional Triggers: Certain feelings which consist of fear, tension, anger, or disappointment also can motive people to relive the worrying revel in or have interaction in complicated behaviors. These feelings often replicate feelings skilled during the trauma itself.

Chapter 2: Breaking the Stigma

The Stigma Surrounding Mental Health

Over the years, mental health troubles have often been misunderstood or unnoticed as a signal of private susceptible factor, and this faulty assumption continues to persist in masses of circles. People with PTSD can face judgement or discrimination based totally at the misconceptions approximately their situation. This wrong notion now not first-rate prevents human beings from on the lookout for help but moreover hinders their adventure within the course of recovery.

To address the stigma surrounding intellectual health, it is vital to educate the general public on what PTSD includes and debunk myths regularly associated with it.

Increased recognition can help human beings recognize that PTSD isn't a flaw in someone's character however as an alternative a psychological scenario that impacts numerous humans at some stage in all walks of life. It can end result from any disturbing event along with herbal disasters, accidents, abuse, or combat research that impact the mind's capacity to tool emotions properly.

One big hurdle in overcoming the stigma round PTSD is that it's miles an invisible pain – its signs might not be obvious to others, contributing to incorrect records and misconception once they display off behaviors which embody anger, tension, or withdrawn dispositions. As a society, we want to foster an surroundings wherein individuals who are experiencing mental demanding situations experience secure to speak approximately them openly with out worry of judgement or shunning.

By encouraging open conversations on highbrow fitness troubles like PTSD, we create possibilities for individuals to are seeking out assist and assist from own family, buddies, and specialists. Acknowledging the severity and legitimacy of PTSD as a real trouble will permit us to debunk stereotypes and promote empathy for those who struggle with this burdensome ailment.

It is important to humanize humans with PTSD and spotlight stories that show off their resilience, courage, and recuperation. By discussing man or woman opinions in the media or organizing network activities, we're capable of assist others understand that people with PTSD are unique people who simply need help to heal and reintegrate into society. When we empathize with those laid low with this mental fitness problem, the stigma dissipates, allowing better care and understanding for all.

Another critical detail of tackling the stigma around PTSD is encouraging people who be anxious through it to are seeking out professional assist. Establishing stable areas and resources for the ones humans can create an surroundings in which they experience cushty discussing their worries without worry of being judged or stigmatized. Mental fitness specialists play a important position in diagnosing and treating PTSD and helping humans regain manipulate of their lives. Early intervention can in the end motive improved effects for the ones stricken by this circumstance.

It is likewise noteworthy that buddies, family humans, and co-human beings need to be nicely-knowledgeable approximately the signs and symptoms and signs of PTSD and comprehend the way to reply successfully whilst a person famous these signs. Supporting cherished ones with the useful resource of lending a listening ear or supplying assist in finding a therapist will move an prolonged way in supporting them manage their highbrow fitness.

Furthermore, volunteer agencies assisting those who be troubled through PTSD can be instrumental in breaking down the limitations that stigma has constructed. Support groups emphasize healing through shared stories, developing a revel in of camaraderie among those who may additionally have felt remoted formerly. These groups foster desire for a brighter destiny – proving that you can regain control in their existence regardless of dealing with PTSD.

Encouraging Open Conversations

The adventure to overcoming PTSD can be a long and exhausting one. It often calls for a sturdy assist device and the braveness to confront past traumas head-on. One of the maximum essential factors of this restoration method is fostering open conversations approximately emotions, mind, and critiques. Encouraging open conversation not only helps humans with PTSD beautify their emotional resilience, however it moreover creates a subculture of know-how that helps restoration and growth.

1. The Importance of Open Conversations: PTSD can leave people feeling remoted, disconnected, and misunderstood. The sheer complexity of feelings and recollections associated with PTSD could make it tough for patients to explicit themselves very well or to discover the proper terms to articulate their reviews.

Open conversations provide an opportunity for human beings with PTSD to find out their feelings and better recognize their research. By sharing brazenly approximately their feelings, mind, and fears, they might start to make feel of their trauma in a context that promotes restoration. Furthermore, open conversations foster deeper connections with others through growing a shared data of the individual's journey via PTSD recuperation.

2. Encouraging Open Conversations with Friends & Family: Friends and circle of relatives contributors won't constantly recognize how extraordinary to assist a person in their journey with PTSD. Honest

communique is important to constructing empathy and expertise amongst loved ones. To create a steady area for communicate:

a) Regularly check in at the man or woman's properly-being.

b) Create moments for connection by the use of setting aside time mainly dedicated to discussing emotions.

c) Avoid making assumptions approximately what they are experiencing; instead, workout energetic listening.

d) Offer validation through maintaining statements like "I pay interest you" or "I'm proper here for you."

e) Ask open-ended questions to permit the individual with PTSD to guide the communication as wished.

f) Encourage them thru acknowledging development, boom, and any fine modifications of their emotions or mind.

2. Encouraging Open Conversations with Professional Support: Mental health professionals play a crucial position in helping human beings with PTSD triumph over their trauma. Communication is excessive in those relationships, so each occasions need to experience snug discussing mind and emotions brazenly. To foster open verbal exchange with highbrow fitness specialists:

a) Clearly articulate desires for treatment classes and talk any concerns.

b) Share development, insights, or setbacks skilled outdoor of treatment classes.

c) Ask questions about the treatment approach, and are seeking rationalization to better recognize the approach.

d) Discuss any feelings that rise up in the end of treatment openly; doing so can help make clear and deal with underlying issues greater successfully.

3. Establishing Safe Spaces: Creating environments that facilitate open verbal

exchange is vital to fostering recuperation for human beings with PTSD. Safe regions offer an surroundings in which people enjoy supported and understood with out the concern of judgment or rejection. Consider putting in solid regions inside:

a) Support groups: Connecting with others who proportion similar evaluations can be empowering and reassuring.

b) School or administrative center settings: By advocating for intellectual fitness hobby and anti-stigma policies, you can help create a supportive surroundings that encourages open conversations approximately PTSD.

c) Community duties: Promote intellectual health consciousness via community sports activities, shows, or workshops.

4. Fighting Stigma: Stigma surrounding PTSD can be a good sized barrier to open conversations about the infection. It is critical to task misconceptions about PTSD by way of the use of manner of sharing accurate

information concerning its signs and signs, reasons, and remedy options. Address stigma thru:

a) Dispelling myths and stereotypes about PTSD thru instructing those round you.

b) Encouraging media portrayals that accurately represent people with PTSD on the identical time as keeping off risky clichés.

c) Advocating for intellectual fitness training internal schools and community communities.

Seeking Help Without Shame

For many those who struggle with PTSD, the very idea of searching out help can experience pretty intimidating. Society tells us that we must be strong enough to deal with our issues on our private. As a quit quit result, humans suffering with PTSD regularly feel ashamed or prone once they bear in mind looking for manual. However, it's essential to recognize that assist-attempting to find isn't always a signal of weak spot – in reality, it suggests massive braveness and strength. The following suggestions are accurate beginning elements for people with PTSD who need to are attempting to find assist:

1. Breaking the Stigma: One of the primary steps in seeking out assist without shame is spotting and tackling the stigma associated with mental health disorders, particularly PTSD. This includes educating ourselves and others approximately what PTSD is, its reasons, and its effect on an character's life. Sharing private tales and tasty in open conversations approximately intellectual fitness permits enhance reputation and assignment misconceptions about intellectual infection.

2. Embracing Vulnerability: Admitting that we want assistance is hard for lots humans because it makes us experience susceptible and uncovered. However, vulnerability is a essential element of recovery, because it permits us to attach deeply with others who can offer manual in the path of our difficult times.

The key's to find out consistent spaces in which you could openly admit your struggles with out worry of judgment or ridicule. This can be a close friend or member of the family you obtain as authentic with or becoming a member of a web or in-man or woman help corporation in which others furthermore percentage their PTSD reports.

3. Recognizing Your Strengths: Instead of focusing in your weaknesses, have a superb time your strengths at the same time as drawing close to help-searching for from this mind-set. Acknowledge the bravery it took on the way to face your trauma head-on and include your plight for recuperation.

By viewing yourself as brave for taking movement inside the course of restoration in preference to inclined for looking help, it turns into a lot less complicated to are looking for for assist with out shame or embarrassment.

four. Acknowledging the Benefits of Therapy: Therapy is an crucial device in PTSD recovery, and seeking out the steering of a professional intellectual health enterprise can lead you on the direction to finding healing. Psychotherapy, EMDR, and cognitive behavioral remedy are a number of the various evidence-based totally techniques used to address PTSD effectively.

Discussing your reviews with a professional professional can offer you with beneficial insights into your signs and symptoms and offer you new coping mechanisms tailor-made in your specific desires. By acknowledging the potential benefits of treatment, searching for professional assist becomes a extra healthful and much much less daunting prospect.

5. Distinguishing Support from Handouts: It is essential to remind yourself that accepting help or seeking out treatment for PTSD does now not equate to taking handouts or charity. Just as a person with a physical harm might possibly go to a scientific health practitioner for assist, so must someone struggling with

PTSD are seeking out help from intellectual health specialists or others who've been via similar critiques.

6. Dispelling Fear of Rejection: In a few instances, human beings may additionally additionally moreover avoid on the lookout for assist due to the fact they fear they'll no longer be taken significantly or might be rejected with the aid of these they flip to for assist. This problem is definitely legitimate; but, it is important now not to permit this worry to save you you from pursuing vital help.

Chapter 3: Seeking Professional Help

The Importance of Professional Treatment

When a person critiques a disturbing occasion, it is able to have extended-lasting mental effects. Many humans also can attempt to cope and go with the flow in advance, but the lingering strain and anxiety can come to be overwhelming at times. This is in which expert treatment for PTSD comes into play. It gives targeted manual and guidance especially designed for human beings struggling with PTSD.

One of the number one benefits of seeking out professional manual is that the ones practitioners are knowledgeable to become privy to the inspiration motives of your PTSD.

They apprehend a way to get to the coronary heart of your trauma and manual you via a restoration approach based totally on proof-primarily based therapeutic practices. While without a doubt absolutely everyone's needs will vary, a professional therapist can create a customized treatment plan that works first-class for you.

Another advantage of on the lookout for expert assistance is that it gives a consistent space for people to discover their feelings, feelings, and memories. Trying to navigate thru this form of complex restoration manner for your personal runs the chance of inflicting greater emotional misery or maybe re-traumatization – an enjoy in which the character relives their trauma, inflicting further damage to their highbrow fitness. A expert therapist helps lessen the ones risks and maintains the method transferring in the right course.

Professional therapists additionally have access to current studies in PTSD remedy methodologies. By staying contemporary with new discoveries and strategies in their issue, they may be able to adapt treatment plans through the years to ensure powerful improvement. This turns into especially crucial as new treatments emerge that might offer higher results than traditional techniques.

Moreover, social useful resource plays a critical characteristic in overcoming trauma-associated demanding conditions. Professional therapists apprehend how crucial it is to enhance relationships among customers and their help networks — be it own family individuals or buddies who offer encouragement and information. Incorporating first-class interpersonal interactions inner remedy training contributes to the fulfillment of overcoming PTSD.

Treatment for PTSD is extra than surely talking about events that took place within the past. Professionals make use of severa assets and skills-constructing strategies to help patients higher deal with every day existence. For example, one not unusual technique is Cognitive-Behavioral Therapy (CBT), which allows people understand horrible idea styles and increase more wholesome coping mechanisms. Another notably-used technique is Eye Movement Desensitization and Reprocessing (EMDR), which permits customers to device demanding memories as a manner to heal from their outcomes.

These techniques, among others, are vital in supporting people locate the excellent route to recovery. The expert steerage and manual provided for the duration of therapy enhance the possibilities of efficaciously overcoming PTSD.

It's important to understand that the journey to overcome PTSD is not a one-length-fits-all way. Professionals renowned this and utilize severa techniques, along side CBT and EMDR, to tailor their guide to each client's unique wishes and desires. Furthermore, they prioritize protection and emotional well-being in some unspecified time in the future of therapy durations, assisting human beings navigate their recuperation course without inflicting in addition damage.

Another critical problem of expert treatment is spotting the significance of self-care outdoor of treatment. Professionals can guide clients in identifying sports sports that promote relaxation, strain cut price, and everyday emotional properly-being. Incorporating mindfulness practices which incorporates meditation or undertaking pursuits can also make a contribution extensively to healing achievement.

Finding the Right Therapist

It is vital for people to discover a therapist who isn't always most effective professional however additionally an exact sufficient in form for his or her goals and options. Here are a few key factors to bear in mind while seeking out a therapist:

1. Determine your dreams: Before starting your search for a therapist, you need to have a smooth records of what you need in terms of assist and knowledge. Consider the following questions:

a) What form of therapy may additionally first-class in form my desires? (e.G., Cognitive Behavioral Therapy (CBT), Eye Movement Desensitization and Reprocessing (EMDR), Psychodynamic Therapy)

b) Do I require a trauma-targeted professional or a greater generalized therapist?

c) Would I determine upon a certified mental health professional or an authorized peer counselor who has experienced PTSD themselves?

2. Do your research: Once you understand your options, start reading ability therapists on your area who consciousness on PTSD remedy. Consult databases like Psychology Today or close by resource organizations to

find out specialists with the famous credentials.

three. Read reviews: Client testimonials can be precious whilst considering whether or not or not the therapist might be an top notch in shape for you. Keep in thoughts that everybody's revel in is specific, so it is important not to rely too closely on opinions on my own.

four. Check qualifications: Make effective the potential therapist holds appropriate licensure for their career and region of specialization. You can generally find this data on their internet net web page or by means of accomplishing out right away.

5. Schedule an preliminary session: Many therapists offer loose consultations both through way of cell telephone or in-man or woman, permitting you to invite essential questions and gauge your consolation level with them earlier than committing to ongoing lessons.

6. Assess compatibility: During your initial session, be privy to how properly you connect to the therapist on both a personal and expert degree.

a) Are they easy to speak to and do they devise a stable area for sharing your critiques?

b) Are their verbal exchange fashion and method properly acceptable along side your goals?

c) Do they specialize in the kind of treatment you want and offer evidence-primarily based treatment for PTSD?

7. Discuss logistics: Ensure that the therapist's availability, workplace vicinity, and expenses align together at the side of your goals. Many therapists provide sliding scale charges or paintings with insurance carriers.

eight. Monitor development: Once you begin remedy, typically confirm whether or not or no longer it is jogging for you. Are you making progress toward your desires? Bring up any issues in-session to facilitate open talk and changes as crucial.

9. Be affected man or woman: Healing from PTSD may be a lengthy technique, and the proper therapist might be a critical detail of your recuperation journey. Commit to giving your therapeutic relationship time to increase and reframing setbacks as possibilities for growth.

10. Don't be afraid to replace therapists: If you enjoy that your cutting-edge therapist isn't always the right healthy, do no longer hesitate to are seeking out for opportunity manual. Not all therapists can be suitable to every body, and it is essential to prioritize locating the right character who contributes undoubtedly closer to your restoration and healing.

Exploring Therapy Options

The road to recovery from PTSD may be complicated and full of uncertainty, however it's miles essential to recall which you are not by myself. With the right useful resource tool and treatment alternatives, you may overcome PTSD and regain manipulate over your life. There are diverse remedy strategies available for treating PTSD, and some people can also additionally advantage from combining virtually certainly one of a kind styles of treatment. Key remedy options embody:

1. Cognitive-Behavioral Therapy: It is a appreciably-used healing approach that makes a speciality of changing concept styles and behaviors. For human beings with PTSD, CBT can assist discover triggers for anxiety and negative feelings, and educate wholesome coping mechanisms. This can encompass addressing self-blame or guilt regularly professional through trauma survivors. CBT generally includes character periods among the affected person and therapist.

2. Prolonged Exposure Therapy: It is a selected shape of CBT designed for those laid

low with PTSD. The treatment involves dealing with the traumatic reminiscence in a managed environment at the same time as running along a professional therapist. The approach consists of grade by grade revisiting the annoying event in small increments to reduce anxiety round those recollections and feelings. Over time, sufferers will discover themselves less reactive and better equipped to control their symptoms.

three. Eye Movement Desensitization and Reprocessing: It is an evidence-based totally totally remedy mainly designed for human beings with PTSD. EMDR combines elements of exposure treatment with techniques that incorporate bilateral stimulation (the use of eye actions, auditory tones, or tactile stimulation). Throughout the way, sufferers recognition on their worrying memories on the identical time as simultaneously experiencing bilateral stimulation from the therapist. This allows re-gadget the stressful experience in a healthy manner, allowing new neural connections to shape in dealing with the distressing memories.

4. Trauma-focused Cognitive Processing Therapy: It is any other effective remedy preference specific to PTSD. This shape of treatment specializes in addressing the ideals and idea patterns that upward push up because of the trauma. The therapist works with the affected man or woman to understand maladaptive mind, discover options, and increase extra wholesome methods to address and reframe their annoying opinions.

Chapter 4: Self-Help Strategies for Coping

Mindfulness and Grounding Techniques

Mindfulness is defined due to the fact the act of consciously focusing one's interest on the present 2nd in a non-judgmental way, this means that that during preference to getting caught up in horrible thoughts approximately the beyond or future, an person is handiest centered at the triumphing. In the context of PTSD, mindfulness practices offer a manner to navigate beyond the annoying recollections with the useful useful resource of cultivating an hobby of the prevailing moment. Key advantages of mindfulness workout:

Reduced strain and anxiety stages

Improved emotional law

Enhanced highbrow readability and consciousness

Increased self-interest

Enhanced resilience in dealing with annoying recollections

There are numerous sorts of mindfulness practices appropriate for individuals dealing with PTSD:

1.   Breath-focused meditation: A fundamental mindfulness exercise that entails that specialize in one's breath because it flows in and out of the frame.

2.   Body scan meditation: This exercise consists of systematically that specialize in brilliant additives of one's body at the identical time as watching sensations without judgment.

three. Loving-kindness meditation: A compassion-primarily based exercise in which individuals deliver top notch energy to themselves and others through repetitive terms along side "May I be glad, can also I be nicely."

4. Guided imagery meditation: This entails visualizing non violent, calming pix or conditions to help recognition one's hobby on a serene surroundings.

Grounding stands for reconnecting oneself with fact and anchoring oneself to it through sensory perception or mental sporting occasions. These strategies allow an character to distance oneself from overwhelming feelings related to a stressful occasion, imparting a good buy-desired consolation from PTSD symptoms like flashbacks or dissociation. Key blessings of grounding techniques:

Reinforcing a experience of protection

Reduced anxiety and panic attacks

Improved revel in of manage over one's feelings

Strengthened connection to the prevailing second

There are number one lessons of grounding strategies—sensory grounding and intellectual grounding.

1. Sensory Grounding:

a) The five-four-3-2-1 method: This technique entails identifying five assets you likely can see, 4 matters you'll be able to contact, three subjects you could sincerely pay interest, matters one must heady scent, and one problem one ought to taste.

b) Breathing bodily activities: Deep, slow breaths via the nose whilst concentrating at the sensations experienced in the end of inhalation and exhalation.

c) Tactile grounding: Touching numerous gadgets can prompt a sensation of relatability to the prevailing moment.

2. Mental Grounding:

a) Mindful hobby: One can remember their current surroundings, that specialize in out of doors realities in desire to inner thoughts and sensations.

b) Cognitive wearing activities: Solving intellectual puzzles or video video games redirects interest again to the triumphing second and far from worrying memories.

c) Reciting affirmations: Quoting extremely good affirmations which encompass "I am safe," or "I am robust" makes it much less complicated for an person to reconnect with their current united states of america.

Breathing Exercises for Anxiety

Breathing is an critical part of our lives, and maximum of the time, we do it with out even thinking about it. However, in the path of moments of tension or at the same time as grappling with PTSD, your respiratory may emerge as shallow and less effective. This can inadvertently growth signs and symptoms and symptoms in conjunction with restlessness, feeling annoying, or perhaps experiencing panic assaults. One manner to counteract this trouble is thru running closer to unique respiratory carrying sports. These techniques can help create a experience of calm, alter the fearful device, and alleviate anxiety. Below, we are able to introduce a few effective however smooth respiratory physical sports that you may put into effect into your each day existence.

1. Diaphragmatic Breathing: Diaphragmatic breathing, also called belly breathing, involves using the diaphragm muscle to tug air deep into the lungs. This workout encourages complete oxygen change, slows the coronary heart beat, and allows stabilize blood stress.

a) Begin via finding a cushty function, either sitting or mendacity down.

b) Place one hand in your pinnacle chest and the alternative on your belly.

c) Take a sluggish and deep breath in through your nostril for about four seconds, permitting your stomach to upward push as air fills your lungs.

d) Gently exhale through pursed lips for about six seconds while maintaining the hand for your chest as nevertheless as possible.

e) Repeat this way for severa mins till you revel in extra cushty.

2. Four-7-8 Breathing Technique: The four-7-eight respiration technique is another effective approach to lessen anxiety and promote relaxation rapid. By focusing on this specific pattern of breathing in and exhaling, you may stimulate the relaxation reaction on your frame.

a) Sit in an upright characteristic together together with your once more right away.

b) Close your eyes and let loose a deep exhale through your mouth.

c) Close your mouth and inhale quietly via your nose for 4 counts.

d) Hold your breath for seven counts.

e) Exhale slowly thru your mouth for 8 counts.

f) Repeat the cycle 4 times.

three. Box Breathing: Box respiration, moreover known as four-square respiratory, is a manner often utilized by Navy SEALs to preserve focus and composure within the route of immoderate-strain situations. This workout can assist reduce anxiety with the aid of guiding you to attention in your breath and achieve a relaxed country.

a) Sit or lie down in a cushty feature.

b) Close your eyes and take a deep breath in, then exhale completely.

c) Inhale slowly via your nose for 4 counts.

d) Hold your breath for four counts.

e) Exhale slowly through your mouth for four counts.

f) Finally, preserve your breath another time for 4 counts earlier than repeating the cycle.

4. Alternate Nostril Breathing: This yoga-based method includes alternating the nostrils within the route of inhalation and exhalation, which allows to balance the worried machine and reduce anxiety.

a) Sit in a snug position along facet your backbone immediately.

b) Close your right nostril using your thumb, then inhale slowly through the left nose.

c) Close the left nose the use of your ring finger, then open the right nostril and exhale slowly.

d) Inhale thru the proper nostril at the same time as maintaining the left one closed.

e) Close the proper nostril and exhale thru the left nose.

f) Repeat this machine for several minutes.

five. Resonant Breathing: Resonant respiratory is a way designed to in form our frame's natural rhythms with our breath, selling rest and decreased tension.

a) Find a snug position to sit or lie down.

b) Breathe in deeply for 5 seconds at the equal time as focusing on growing your stomach.

c) Slowly exhale for 5 seconds, allowing all anxiety to head away your body as you bought this.

d) Maintain a slow and consistent rhythm of respiratory for several minutes.

Incorporate those 5 respiratory carrying sports activities into your every day habitual to assist manipulate anxiety and PTSD signs and signs correctly. With normal exercise, you could phrase a large improvement for your highbrow nicely-being as you regain control over your thoughts and emotions. Remember, the most essential hassle of these wearing sports is consistency – making them a part of your each day everyday is essential for lengthy-time period success in overcoming tension.

Journaling for Emotional Release

In our ongoing struggle with PTSD, finding powerful coping strategies is important for the recovery technique. One such technique that has received large attention is journaling for emotional launch. Many people who've navigated the turbulent waters of PTSD have placed solace in setting their thoughts down on paper.

The act of writing lets in us to untangle and confront the emotions that can be overwhelming us. When we magazine with goal, we create a safe region for addressing our thoughts, emotions, and reviews without fear of judgment or outdoor repercussions. It enables us benefit popularity and expertise of our emotions whilst providing an possibility for self-expression and release.

One of the motives journaling is so effective in managing PTSD is that it permits us to reframe annoying reminiscences. By giving ourselves permission to discover those memories brazenly, we're capable of begin to dismantle their have an effect on over our minds. Additionally, journaling allows higher verbal exchange among one-of-a-kind factors of the mind. Following a disturbing occasion, there is usually a disconnect among the emotional areas and those chargeable for processing language. When we write about our research, we integrate those features and promote intellectual healing.

When embarking on journaling as a manner to conquer PTSD, bear in mind the following recommendations:

1. Choose a medium that feels cushty: Some humans determine on typing on a pc or pill, while others discover solace in the use of pen and paper. Consider any accessibility desires as nicely on the same time as making your choice.

Chapter 5: Rebuilding Relationships

Navigating Relationship Challenges

Relationships may be a delivery of pride and achievement; however, additionally they gift stressful situations that every companions need to navigate together. This is mainly real for individuals who've professional trauma and are residing with PTSD. Navigating the landscape of relationship stressful conditions on the equal time as operating thru PTSD is a complex and touchy task, however one this is essential to fostering a wholesome, supportive partnership.

The first step in addressing the effect of PTSD on relationships knows the sickness itself.

PTSD can rise up in numerous strategies, which includes intense emotions of worry, sadness, or anger. This emotional depth could make it hard for some human beings to simply accept as actual with others and shape bonds, at the same time as others may moreover come to be overly reliant on their companions for help. External stimuli can cause flashbacks or emotional reactions that would appear disproportionate to people without PTSD, primary to misunderstandings and frustration. By acknowledging the presence of PTSD of their lives, couples can circulate in advance with empathy and knowledge.

Effective communication is crucial whilst navigating dating annoying situations stemming from PTSD. Being open and honest approximately feelings, triggers, and boundaries will permit each companions to growth a deeper understanding of every certainly one of a type's studies and create an surroundings conducive to restoration. Couples should exercise lively listening –

giving undivided interest without interrupting or judging – in addition to expressing oneself virtually and concisely.

The associate with out PTSD need to be aware that their cherished one's emotional reactions might be excessive or seem out of context. It is critical for them to widely diagnosed these reactions as actual and understand that they stem from trauma in location of deliberately hurtful conduct. Patience, assist, and reassurance are key factors in providing consolation in these moments.

For the person with PTSD, know-how their companion's mind-set is important as well. Recognizing that they may no longer certainly recognize your enjoy lets in for patience at the same time as they're seeking to useful useful resource you emotionally. Sharing belongings about PTSD, in addition to discussing coping mechanisms, can assist each companions better recognize and help one another.

Couples also can remember implementing a "solid word" or sign that the partner with PTSD can use even as feeling crushed or brought about. This communique device can allow for candid conversations and permit the alternative companion to offer immediate aid.

Maintaining a wholesome balance of connection and independence can be hard for couples tormented by PTSD, however it's far vital to maintain man or woman identities and private growth. Encourage each other to pursue pastimes, socialize with pals, or participate in diverse sports activities. Promoting independence allows each partner to grow in my opinion and attain private goals whilst continuing to assist every distinct's mental fitness journey collectively.

Professional counseling can provide guidance even as navigating dating stressful situations stemming from PTSD. Couples treatment with a mental fitness professional professional in trauma-related problems can offer precious gadget for expertise triggers, working toward effective conversation, and growing strategies for assisting every distinct during tough moments. In addition, counseling training can assist foster an environment of accept as actual with, fostering emotional healing for each partners.

Prioritizing self-care is vital for retaining a healthful relationship while dealing with PTSD. Engage in activities that promote bodily health which incorporates exercising, right sufficient sleep, and balanced vitamins. Furthermore, domesticate self-soothing sports which consist of meditation, rest strategies, or journaling.

One important issue of self-care is warding off isolation. Connecting with others who are also managing PTSD thru aid companies or online groups gives an possibility for collective recovery and camaraderie. By sharing stories, imparting peer guide, and presenting choice for the future to others experiencing comparable annoying situations creates precious bonds.

Finally, remember that recovery is a way that takes effort and time from each companions. Be organized for setbacks and keep right away to the perception that healing is possible. Stay devoted to non-public increase and remind your self of the resilience which you possess in overcoming relationship demanding conditions.

Communicating with Loved Ones

PTSD impacts no longer simplest the person who has professional demanding sports but moreover their loved ones. Close relationships can be strained as human beings with PTSD war to talk effectively, revel in emotional outbursts, or withdraw from social conditions. This section highlights strategies for beginning and retaining channels of communique with loved ones even as on the adventure to overcoming PTSD.

1. Establishing trust: Building be given as genuine with amongst you and the one you love with PTSD is vital for effective conversation. Make positive to create a stable

place in which they may be capable of particular themselves openly with out worry of judgment or misconception. To construct bear in mind:

a) Be reliable: Keep your ensures, be consistent, and examine via on agreements.

b) Be sincere: Share your feelings and thoughts simply whilst discussing topics related to PTSD.

c) Demonstrate empathy: Listen actively and validate their feelings through recognizing their stressful conditions and ache.

three. Active listening: Effective conversation calls for active listening abilities honed through running inside the course of patience, empathy, and openness. To practice active listening:

a) Maintain eye contact: Establishing eye contact suggests that you are actually interested in what the one that you love has to say.

b) Provide undivided hobby: Avoid distractions so you can cognizance on facts the one you love's feelings.

c) Ask open-ended questions: Encourage them to share their mind or make easy unresolved problems.

d) Reflect lower lower back what you understand: Paraphrase their speech and ask if you understood correctly; this shows that you are paying hobby and on the lookout for to understand their emotions.

4. Use 'I' statements: 'I' statements precise your feelings with out escalating the state of affairs with the aid of way of blaming or accusing the one that you love. They foster a more notable talk and sell know-how. For instance, in preference to pronouncing, "You never proportion your feelings with me," try "I enjoy damage and disconnected at the identical time as we do not talk about our emotions."

5. Encourage appropriate expression of feelings: While it's far essential for humans with PTSD to precise their emotions, it is also crucial that they discover ways to particular themselves constructively. Encourage the only that you like to share their feelings without resorting to anger or aggression.

6. Discuss triggers and coping mechanisms: Talking approximately triggers allow you to each perceive early warning symptoms and symptoms and avoid situations that could exacerbate PTSD signs and symptoms. Discuss coping mechanisms and understand which techniques paintings amazing for your beloved.

7. Set boundaries: Establishing smooth boundaries and expectancies protects each you and your beloved from emotional harm. Clearly talk what behaviors are suitable and unacceptable, emphasizing that the ones barriers are important for maintaining a wholesome dating.

8. Seek expert help: A intellectual health expert can assist the only that you love study powerful verbal exchange system. Consider attending therapy periods together to enhance the bond amongst you and discuss traumatic conditions in a safe environment guided by means of the usage of an expert.

nine. Practice self-care: Managing your very very personal strain is important in helping someone with PTSD correctly. Engage in self-care sports which includes workout, meditation, or looking for assist from buddies or experts to make certain which you stay the compassionate and affected character listener the only that you love desires.

10. Be affected man or woman: Recovery from PTSD is not immediate, as it calls for time and dedication from every the character struggling and their aid device. Understand that improvement is probably slow but extensive improvement may be made with staying energy, know-how, and steady communique.

Reconnecting and Reestablishing Trust

Reestablishing believe is a crucial element of rebuilding relationships after experiencing PTSD. Trust is the muse for any wholesome bond; eventually, incorporating the subsequent strategies can nurture its regrowth.

1. Be regular: Consistency is prime in demonstrating your reliability for your own family. This entails now not best making commitments however also following via with them. Maintain a everyday presence in their lives thru showing up when they need you and standing by using manner of your ensures. Through reliability, agree with may be regained, allowing you both to develop in tandem.

2. Rebuild intimacy: Intimacy isn't pretty much closeness on a bodily degree however additionally consists of developing emotional connections. Engage in sports that sell bonding together along with your associate, which encompass attending couples' remedy

or gambling leisure sports activities collectively. Approach rebuilding emotional and bodily intimacy often; keep away from dashing or pressuring every different as your connection deepens. Remember that a sturdy basis will motive prolonged-lasting consequences.

3. Apologize even as crucial: PTSD-associated struggles can once in a while motive damage in relationships. In these instances, it is vital which you take obligation to your moves and offer a real apology to everyone affected. Own as much as any mistakes made throughout this time, notwithstanding the fact that they have been no longer intentional. An actual expression of remorse can go with the flow a long manner in rebuilding be given as true with amongst companions.

Chapter 6: Overcoming Nightmares and Flashbacks

Understanding Nightmares and Flashbacks

As we close to our eyes and go with the flow into the vicinity of sleep, our unconscious comes alive with particular pictures, emotions, and narratives. It is in the route of the REM (Rapid Eye Movement) section of sleep that nightmares can happen. For human beings laid low with PTSD, the ones nightmares function an unwelcome reminder of the traumas they have got professional in their lives. The seemingly limitless cycle of reliving the most excruciating moments can make it difficult to discover solace even in slumber.

It is quite not unusual for PTSD-associated nightmares to examine a habitual pattern with the identical conditions, humans, or emotions gambling out in every nocturnal visitation. The sheer vividness and terror of these dreams can cause giant misery for the ones affected. As a result, sleep styles can be notably disrupted, main to emotional exhaustion or fear surrounding falling asleep.

But why do such nightmares get up? The clinical clarification within the lower back of this phenomenon stems from how traumatized people device memories. Their brains generally conflict to system disturbing reminiscences in an organized manner at some stage in sleep, thereby causing those nightmarish intrusions.

While nightmares haunt sufferers in the course in their sleep, flashbacks offer no respite even when one is aware. These intrusive recollections of past trauma can emerge into one's focus, relentlessly confronting people with their most painful studies. Flashbacks are mainly misleading – they will sense so actual that one must accept as true with they're reliving their trauma in that very second.

The impact flashbacks have on PTSD patients extends beyond mere emotional distress, as human beings stuck in the grip of a flashback can revel in bodily reactions too. These can consist of speedy heartbeat, sweating, trembling, shortness of breath, or perhaps nausea. For many, the overpowering nature of flashbacks effects in avoidance behaviors where humans or situations associated with beyond traumas are consciously skirted.

Perhaps the maximum troubling thing of flashbacks is their unpredictability. Triggers can range from precise sensory cues - like excellent smells or sounds - to extra abstract stimuli, which incorporates specific phrases or emotions. This unpredictability leaves folks who enjoy flashbacks feeling continuously susceptible and on component.

Coping Strategies for Nightmares

Nightmares can be distressing critiques, mainly for folks that be afflicted through PTSD. The remarkable, regularly terrifying conditions can feel all too actual, making it difficult to find solace and enjoy secure even within the consolation of 1's mattress. In this segment, we are able to find out various coping strategies that will help you manipulate and reduce the frequency and depth of nightmares, ultimately imparting a more restful sleep revel in.

1. Establish a Bedtime Routine: Creating a constant bedtime ordinary can help sign your frame that it is time for sleep. Aim for calming sports activities, which incorporates studying or taking a warmth tub in advance than mattress. Relaxing rituals can assist lessen strain and tension degrees, that would make a contribution to nightmares.

2. Create a Sleep-Inviting Environment: Anxiety may be caused by the usage of way of a chaotic or demanding surroundings, so it is important to create a calming surroundings to your bed room. Remove any useless distractions (which encompass electronics) and preserve a clean, prepared place. Soft lights, cushty bedding, and soothing scents (which includes lavender) can contribute to developing emotions of calm and relaxation.

3. Practice Relaxation Techniques: Incorporate rest techniques into your bedtime ordinary to help reduce strain and anxiety levels before sleep. Deep respiration wearing sports activities, contemporary-day muscle rest, meditation, or guided imagery can all assist you transition right right into a extra snug nation of mind.

4. Maintain a Healthy Lifestyle: Maintaining accurate physical fitness is essential in selling better sleep excellent and might help lessen the intensity or frequency of nightmares. Incorporate everyday exercise into your every

day regular (preferably in advance in the day), devour well-balanced food (averting heavy or quite spiced dishes near bedtime), restriction caffeine and alcohol intake (which also can disrupt sleep), and avoid nicotine.

five. Keep a Sleep Diary: A sleep diary can be a beneficial device for tracking any styles or capability triggers on your nightmares. Record whilst you visit mattress, whilst you awaken, how regularly you enjoy nightmares, and another applicable facts. By studying this data, you and your healthcare professional can paintings together to emerge as aware of any styles or contributing factors that can be exacerbating your nightmare opinions.

6. CBT for Nightmares: It is an effective treatment opportunity that has been confirmed to help reduce nightmares in humans with PTSD. During commands, a informed therapist will assist you understand concept patterns that make a contribution to nightmares and train you techniques to cope with them. Imagery exercise consultation

therapy (IRT), a particular sort of CBT regularly used to cope with nightmares, consists of reimagining and rewriting the completing of a habitual nightmare on the same time as massive wide conscious, in the long run principal to less distressing desires.

7. Medication Options: In a few instances, medicine may be advocated as a part of a comprehensive treatment plan. Antidepressants and antianxiety medicinal capsules can doubtlessly help beautify sleep amazing and reduce nightmares for a few humans with PTSD. Always are searching out advice from a certified healthcare professional in advance than starting or enhancing any medicine ordinary.

eight. Support Networks: Connecting with others who've professional comparable stressful situations can be pretty useful in dealing with PTSD-associated nightmares. Support corporations, on-line forums, or treatment groups can offer precious insight and statistics from others who've confronted similar issues. Additionally, buddies and circle of relatives members may be vital resources of emotional assist sooner or later of tough instances.

nine. Develop Coping Mechanisms: Identify coping mechanisms that artwork notable for you even as managing anxiety or distress related to nightmares. This should possibly involve in search of consolation from a cherished one, conducting grounding techniques (which incorporates deep breathing physical sports), schooling self-compassion, or repeating outstanding affirmations.

10. Seeking Professional Help: If your nightmares are considerably impacting your splendid of lifestyles or fitness, it's miles vital to gain out for professional assist from a highbrow health expert. A licensed therapist can provide steerage on appropriate coping techniques based to your character goals and research.

Taking rate of your sleep revel in and imposing those coping techniques can assist promote better sleep awesome and reduce the frequency and depth of nightmares. This, in turn, can make contributions to everyday upgrades in intellectual fitness and nicely-being, permitting you to transport ahead towards a more enjoyable life. Remember that overcoming nightmares associated with PTSD might be a slow approach, so be affected person with your self and function a laugh your improvement along the manner.

Managing Flashbacks in Daily Life

Flashbacks can be one of the most tough and debilitating signs and symptoms of PTSD. They can arise at any given second, leaving you feeling disoriented, overwhelmed, and no longer able to characteristic. Let's explore severa strategies that will help you control flashbacks in each day existence, permitting you to regain manipulate and paintings closer to residing a more fulfilled existence.

1. Recognize your triggers: The first step in handling flashbacks is to become privy to what triggers them. This might not commonly be an smooth challenge, as triggers may be subtle or deeply buried within the unconscious mind. To recognize those triggers, be aware of outside elements, feelings, or thoughts simply in advance than a flashback takes vicinity. Keep a journal to file those observations and look for styles that could indicate what provokes your flashbacks.

2. Develop grounding techniques: Grounding techniques are essential gear for dealing with flashbacks. They assist you come to the triumphing 2d and disengage from the overwhelming emotions skilled at some point of a flashback. Some of the best grounding techniques encompass:

Chapter 7: Healing From Within

Self-Care and Self-Compassion

Self-care is the exercise of prioritizing your bodily, emotional, and intellectual nicely-being via active engagement in sports activities that promote not unusual fitness. When enhancing from PTSD, self-care permits in lowering strain levels, improving resilience, and promoting healing. Here are a few self-care practices that permit you to on this hard route:

1. Sleep: Give yourself permission to rest. Aim for a everyday sleep schedule with 7-9 hours of sleep ordinary with night time time. Establish a bedtime recurring that promotes

relaxation and a sleep-conducive environment.

2. Nutrition: Nourish your body with balanced nutrients and live hydrated. Consume masses of whole meals rich in nutrients, nutrients, and minerals that assist help number one body feature and immune device fitness.

3. Exercise: Engage in regular physical hobby that you enjoy, in conjunction with strolling, swimming, or yoga. Exercise can help regulate mood with the useful resource of freeing endorphins on the same time as lowering cortisol levels.

4. Relaxation strategies: Find time to loosen up every day using techniques which include deep-breathing exercises, mindfulness meditation, or modern muscle relaxation. These practices can help calm your fearful machine and reduce strain tiers.

five. Social connections: Maintain supportive relationships with buddies, circle of relatives individuals, or assist businesses who recognize the demanding situations you face.

6. Creative expression: Engage in creative shops like journaling, portray, or gambling an device that permits for emotional expression at the same time as fostering feelings of accomplishment and private growth.

In addition to self-care practices that benefit your physical and emotional fitness, it is essential now not to overlook the importance of self-compassion in some unspecified time within the future of your recuperation journey. Self-compassion includes treating your self with kindness, statistics, and forgiveness. It encourages one to be their private super buddy, particularly while coping with issues and setbacks. Why is self-compassion important at some point of PTSD recovery?

1. Reduces self-blame: PTSD symptoms and symptoms can purpose emotions of guilt, disgrace, and self-blame. Practicing self-compassion allows you to understand that

your emotions and reactions are not your fault however as an opportunity a reaction to a demanding experience.

2. Encourages persistence: Healing from PTSD takes time and might contain setbacks along the way. Being compassionate closer to yourself encourages staying energy with the manner, helping you preserve wish and determination notwithstanding troubles.

three. Enhances self-reputation: Self-compassion allows you turn out to be extra privy to your mind and feelings, allowing you to apprehend unhelpful belief patterns or coping mechanisms that might keep away from your development.

4. Relieves emotional distress: Acknowledging and validating hard feelings without judgment fosters recuperation, making it a whole lot much less difficult to allow flow of ache and flow ahead at the route to restoration.

How are you capable of workout self-compassion?

1. Be aware of terrible self-speak: Listen for vital or hurtful thoughts directed in the direction of your self. Challenge those mind with kindness and records, specializing inside the large photograph of your restoration journey.

2. Forgive yourself for mistakes: Remind your self that setbacks are a part of increase and restoration. Do now not stay on regrets however as an alternative view them as learning possibilities for improvement.

3. Celebrate development: Recognize and feature fun non-public improvements made at some point of your recuperation machine — regardless of how small they will appear.

four. Practice gratitude: Regularly taking time to explicit gratitude for what is going nicely for your life can foster a extra exceptional mind-set.

5. Reach out for assist: Connect with depended on friends, circle of relatives individuals, or therapists who can help remind

you to be gentle with your self inside the direction of hard moments.

Incorporating self-care and self-compassion practices into your each day routine is a vital component of any PTSD recovery plan. Prioritizing your properly-being, treating yourself kindly, and accepting that imperfections are part of the recovery way, will empower you to retain overcoming the annoying situations that PTSD gives.

Reconnecting with Your Body

The journey to overcoming PTSD is difficult and, at times, can enjoy overwhelming. In our quest for restoration, we often attention on the intellectual and emotional factors of recuperation on the equal time as neglecting our physical our our our bodies. But the reality is, reconnecting collectively with your body is an important difficulty of overcoming PTSD and embracing a extra match, balanced lifestyles. Here, we are able to discover various strategies that will help you recognize and befriend your body as you development through the PTSD recovery method.

1. Mindful Awareness of the Body: One of the strategies to reconnect together collectively along with your body is thru working towards aware interest. This method consists of bringing your whole hobby to severa elements of your body without judgment, permitting you to increase a deeper connection to your physical sensations.

To practice aware consciousness, find out a quiet and cushty area wherein you may sit down or lie down with out distractions. Begin through taking numerous deep breaths, breathing in thru your nostril and exhaling through your mouth. As you try this, try to allow go of any tensions or thoughts that may be occupying your mind. Next, recognition your interest on specific regions of your frame, beginning in conjunction with your toes and step by step shifting upward to consist of each part of yourself. Feel any sensations that could exist in each location with out seeking to adjust them or decide their importance.

2. Progressive Muscle Relaxation: PMR is a way designed particularly to reduce tension inside the frame. It includes tightening one-of-a-type muscle organizations for a few seconds earlier than releasing the anxiety in a managed way.

To practice PMR, begin at one surrender of your body (each the top or toes) and systematically paintings through every muscle organization till you bought the opportunity quit. First, disturbing every muscle group for approximately five seconds on the same time as that specialize in the way it feels. Then release the anxiety for approximately twenty seconds, listening to how the feeling modifications from tenseness to relaxation.

3. Grounding Techniques: Grounding techniques are designed to help you hook up with the prevailing second thru engaging your physical senses. This results in a shift in awareness a ways from the thoughts and

feelings that contribute to your PTSD signs and symptoms and signs. Examples of grounding techniques consist of:

a) Walking barefoot on grass, sand, or soil

b) Holding onto a easy stone or every other comforting item

c) Connecting with the smells of nature – flora, trees, or freshly cut grass

d) Listening to soothing track or the herbal sounds spherical you

four. Somatic Experiencing: It is a healing approach that makes a speciality of releasing trauma stored inside the frame through direct physical engagement. SE practitioners paintings with you to grow to be aware about and launch bodily stuck styles and sell recuperation from both physical and emotional traumas.

5. Body-based totally totally really Practices: Engaging in bodily sports activities sports can extensively decorate your functionality to

reconnect together in conjunction with your body. These bodily video games help alleviate stress, regulate temper, and provide a experience of success as you are making development. Some frame-primarily based totally surely practices to keep in mind encompass:

a) Yoga: The aggregate of bodily postures, respiration wearing activities, and meditation in yoga can bring about profound rest and heightened physical interest.

b) Dance Therapy: Dancing is a super way to unique ourselves nonverbally whilst connecting with our our our bodies.

c) Tai Chi: This martial artwork emphasizes sluggish, flowing moves that domesticate mindfulness and power stability in the frame.

6. Massage Therapy: Massage treatment gives many advantages for humans improving from PTSD via imparting treatment from muscle anxiety, selling relaxation, and organising a deeper connection to as a minimum one's

very own body. If you pick out out to discover rub down remedy as part of your restoration journey, paintings with therapists who're professional in trauma recovery.

As you start incorporating the ones strategies into your every day existence, endure in thoughts that the approach of reconnecting along with your frame is specific for every person. It may also additionally take time, staying power, and regular exercising to foster meaningful alternate. But as you keep your adventure closer to a holistic restoration from PTSD, the reestablishment of a wholesome mind-body connection is a essential issue that can not be overlooked. Embrace the mission, commit to the manner, and have a excellent time within the healing capability that lies inner your non-public frame.

Finding Peace Through Meditation

Life with put up-disturbing pressure sickness (PTSD) can experience like a in no way-finishing war—panic attacks, flashbacks, and the pervading sense of hysteria that might not permit up. Enduring those struggles often takes an intensive emotional toll on one's each day existence. However, amidst the turbulence that PTSD creates, it's far nonetheless viable to find out peace and solace thru the recuperation practice of meditation.

Meditation gives a clean however profound pathway to reconnect with our inner selves on the equal time as little by little restoring stability to our fractured minds. By running toward meditation, we are capable of beef up our resilience and open the door to a greater non violent existence, even within the face of PTSD.

Chapter 8: Coping With Anxiety and Panic

Understanding   Anxiety   in   PTSD

Anxiety is a natural human response that many people revel in even as faced with tough or stressful conditions. It is that feeling of uneasiness or apprehension that arises while we are involved or involved approximately some element. However, excessive and chronic anxiety can emerge as tricky and negatively effect someone's highbrow fitness and properly-being.

When an man or woman has PTSD, their mind may moreover emerge as stuck in a rustic of hyperarousal; this indicates their frame is constantly on immoderate alert for functionality chance or danger. The thoughts's fear center, referred to as the amygdala, becomes overly active at the same time as the prefrontal cortex—accountable for logical thinking and inhibiting emotional responses—turns into underneath-lively. This imbalance in brain hobby in humans with PTSD motives them to perceive threats despite the fact that there are none gift.

Those who be anxious via anxiety associated with PTSD may additionally revel in several bodily, emotional, and cognitive signs and symptoms and signs and symptoms and symptoms. Some of these not unusual manifestations encompass:

1. Excessive Worry: People with PTSD-related anxiety may additionally moreover discover themselves constantly demanding about numerous components of their lives, even if it's miles vain.

2. Avoidance: Individuals can also avoid situations or activities that remind them in

their worrying experience or motive feelings of hysteria. This can bring about social isolation and in all likelihood exacerbate their PTSD signs and symptoms.

3. Hypervigilance: The steady state of immoderate alert could make humans with PTSD extremely sensitive to their surroundings, experiencing a heightened experience of ability threat or hazard.

four. Sleep Disturbances: Anxiety and hyperarousal frequently pass hand-in-hand with sleep issues, which includes insomnia, common awakenings at some stage within the night time time, or nightmares associated with the trauma.

five. Physical Symptoms: Anxiety in PTSD can show up itself via physical sensations inclusive of coronary heart palpitations, dizziness, shortness of breath, trembling, or sweating.

6. Irritability and Mood Swings: The ongoing war among anxiety and stress can go away individuals feeling irritable, having problem

handling emotions, and experiencing unexpected temper modifications.

7. Difficulty Concentrating and Memory Issues: Anxiety related to PTSD will have an impact on someone's cognitive talents and make it extra hard to consciousness on responsibilities or don't forget vital records.

8. Sense of Dread or Impending Doom: From time to time, individuals with tension in PTSD can also additionally sense an splendid sensation of apprehension or fear approximately some element lousy taking vicinity inside the destiny, even if there can be no apparent purpose for it.

As we have seen, tension plays a big position within the lives of people living with PTSD. Understanding its roots and manifestations can offer precious notion into figuring out and addressing the trouble correctly. By looking for professional recommendation from intellectual fitness professionals which includes therapists or psychologists who attention on trauma-associated troubles, humans suffering from anxiety due to their PTSD can discover tailored remedy alternatives that cater to their specific needs.

Techniques for Managing Anxiety

Anxiety is a common and natural response to stress, particularly for human beings residing with PTSD. The "fight or flight" response may be heightened, making it hard to cope with normal conditions. Learning powerful techniques for handling tension can considerably beautify one's high-quality of life.

1. Deep Breathing: When tension moves, our respiratory turns into shallow and fast, which exacerbates the feeling of panic. Practicing deep respiratory wearing sports can help spark off the frame's relaxation response, decreasing anxiety and selling a experience of calm.

a) Find a snug seated function.

b) Slowly breathe in thru your nose for a rely of four.

c) Hold the breath for some exclusive depend of four.

d) Exhale through your mouth for a depend of six.

e) Repeat this sample for several minutes.

2. Progressive Muscle Relaxation: PMR entails tensing and relaxing exceptional muscle agencies inside the frame to release tension, disrupt patterns of hysteria, and promote rest.

a) Start by way of manner of finding a quiet vicinity in which you may sit down or lie down.

b) Tense the muscle businesses in your face through the use of squeezing your eyes close and clenching your jaw.

c) Hold the anxiety for 5 seconds, then launch.

d) Continue running down through each muscle enterprise enterprise:

e) Upper frame: neck, shoulders, top again, palms, palms

f) Torso: chest, stomach

g) Lower frame: buttocks, thighs, calves, toes

h) Hold each muscle contraction for 5 seconds and loosen up for at least 15 seconds earlier than moving directly to the subsequent organization.

three. Cognitive Behavioral Therapy: It is an proof-based remedy demonstrated to be effective in managing tension in people living with PTSD. It specializes in identifying distorted notion patterns that contribute to tension and operating to replace them with greater wholesome options.

a) Consider operating with a skilled therapist professional in CBT to discover the cognitive additives contributing to your anxiety.

b) Develop a list of commonplace concept styles that motive demanding feelings.

c) Work together with your therapist to reframe the ones mind and create more wholesome options.

four. Mindfulness and Meditation: Practicing mindfulness and meditation will let you grow to be greater aware of the winning, preventing anxiety from escalating because of unhelpful mind or feelings.

a) Set apart a couple of minutes every day for quiet mirrored image or meditation.

b) Focus on your respiratory, physical sensations, or gift surroundings without judgment.

c) When stressful mind rise up, exercise acknowledging them without turning into related or judgmental. Allow them to go back lower lower back and bypass like clouds passing via the sky.

five. Maintain Routine: Establishing a every day ordinary can provide structure and predictability for individuals suffering with anxiety associated with PTSD.

a) Plan your day earlier, growing a time desk that consists of self-care, which includes workout, rest strategies, and social sports activities.

b) Keep a constant sleep agenda via going to bed and waking up at comparable times every day.

c) Engage in normal meals and prioritize nourishing food options.

6. Physical Activity: Regular bodily interest can't simplest boom common health however furthermore reduce strain and decorate mood with the aid of using freeing endorphins, known as "feel-right" chemicals within the thoughts.

a) Choose an interesting form of exercising, like strolling, swimming, or yoga.

b) Aim for at the least 1/2-hour of moderate-depth hobby most days of the week.

c) If exercise feels overwhelming, start with shorter intervals and step by step growth the quantity of physical hobby over time.

7. Social Support: Connecting with others who understand your revel in can offer vital assist during times of tension, making it less complicated to manipulate stressors that could stand up from PTSD.

a) Reach out to friends or circle of relatives those who offer fine emotional help.

b) Attend manual companies or therapy intervals with others who've experienced PTSD.

c) Seek out social occasions or golf equipment wherein you may connect to like-minded human beings.

The course to overcoming PTSD and dealing with tension is first rate for every body. Implementing quite a few techniques from this economic disaster will empower you to amplify a customized toolbox for dealing with tension efficaciously. Remember to be affected individual with yourself on this adventure of recovery, and accumulate out for expert manual whilst wanted.

Dealing with Panic Attacks

Panic attacks can occur suddenly and take location with severa bodily and emotional symptoms. Examples of those symptoms and symptoms may moreover furthermore encompass chest pain, shortness of breath, racing heartbeat, dizziness, trembling or shaking, nausea, chills or hot flashes, and a feel of detachment from reality. It is critical to understand those signs so you can nicely deal with them once they arise.

1. Breathing Techniques: One important method to control panic attacks is to cognizance on your respiration. Panic attacks often bring about hyperventilation - taking speedy and shallow breaths which could throw off the steadiness of carbon dioxide in your body. Here are a few physical video games you could strive:

a) Deep stomach respiration: Place a hand for your chest and the possibility in your belly. Inhale slowly through your nose just so only your belly movements. Exhale via your mouth through pursing your lips and ensuring satisfactory your belly moves.

b) four-7-eight method: Inhale thru the nose for 4 counts, maintain your breath for seven counts, exhale through the mouth for 8 counts. Repeat this cycle till the panic attack subsides.

c) Box respiratory: Inhale through the nose for four counts, preserve your breath for four counts, exhale thru the mouth for four counts, maintain an empty breath for some other 4 counts earlier than starting all over again.

Chapter 9: Moving Forward

Setting Personal Goals

It is well-known that a compelling and workable set of personal goals can improve our revel in of reason and allow us to come to be more resilient individuals. As someone embarking on the journey in the direction of restoration from PTSD, setting personal goals is a vital step, one which can effectively map out the direction towards healing. Let us discover the concept of placing personal goals for the ones managing PTSD. In essence, you may learn how to outline realistic goals, prioritize them, damage them down into smaller steps, screen your development over time, and feature an amazing time your achievements.

Before setting any dreams, make the effort to consider what you in reality need in existence. This may also moreover contain envisioning yourself inside the destiny - probable 5 to ten years down the street - and reflecting on what you would like to have finished. Consider your relationships, work, fitness, finances, personal boom and improvement, and your sense of cause.

Once you've got have been given a clean imaginative and prescient of in that you need to move inside the ones center regions of life, jot down unique desires you need to gather. These want to variety from attempting to find a home or beginning a own family to mastering mindfulness strategies or reaching and keeping a healthful weight.

No rely what your chosen goals are for PTSD healing and beyond, they will be more likely to be successful if they agree to the SMART framework:

a) Specific: Your reason desires to be clean and concise - vague or favored thoughts won't assist spur movement or inspire you.

b) Measurable: Quantify your purpose; it should incorporate numbers or probabilities that show display concrete development.

c) Achievable: Set realistic targets based totally to your skills, belongings, and modern-day state of affairs; tough your self is exceptional, but do not cause for some element overly ambitious.

d) Relevant: Ensure your goals in shape into the larger photograph of your PTSD healing plan; inappropriate dreams may also distract in location of assist.

e) Time-sure: Set a time-body for accomplishing your dreams, together with intermittent cut-off dates for measuring development.

Though you can have numerous short- and long-time period goals, it's miles essential to interest on some viable obligations at a time.

Rank those dreams with the useful resource of precedence and commit a while and electricity for this reason.

When you have your prioritized listing of SMART dreams, harm each one down into smaller steps or milestones in an effort to finally bring about their accomplishment. This technique might also need to make massive goals extra capability, growing the danger of success.

Regularly decide your progress inside the route of your goals, reflecting on what is strolling and in which you may in all likelihood need to modify route. It may be beneficial to create movement plans primarily based mostly on timelines, problem-solving techniques, and steps for development.

As you got your milestones and eventually gain your dreams, take a 2d to have a laugh and feature a laugh inside the difficult paintings and resolution it took to get there - regardless of how small the accomplishment can also seem. Acknowledging the ones victories can offer encouragement and motivation to keep pushing beforehand.

Our lives trade continuously, and so do our goals. Don't be afraid to reevaluate or adjust your goal-putting plans as essential. This flexibility is crucial in ensuring that your goals stay relevant for personal boom and recovery.

Lastly, whilst placing private goals related to PTSD recovery particularly, be affected individual with yourself as you embark on this journey. The timeline for recovery varies from man or woman to character; it's far critical no longer to evaluate yourself to others or end up discouraged in case you hit any setbacks.

Instead, keep a increase mindset wherein you look at from the ones setbacks and maintain refining your methods as essential. Focusing on the attempt made in choice to particular effects fosters resilience throughout this hard time.

Chapter 10: Understanding Ptsd In Teens

Definition and Causes of Ptsd In Adolescents

Adolescents can develop Post-Traumatic Stress Disorder (PTSD) in reaction to a annoying occasion they've got professional or witnessed. This can purpose a number distressing signs and symptoms and symptoms that can final for a long term and feature a prime impact on their everyday lifestyles, emotional well-being, and ordinary functioning.

There are severa capacity reasons of PTSD in younger human beings. These encompass direct threats to their existence or bodily integrity, which includes accidents, herbal disasters, bodily or sexual attack, violence, or excessive damage. Abuse or overlook all through formative years, witnessing stressful occasions, battle or warfare, intense injuries or injuries, bullying or harassment, the unexpected lack of lifestyles of a loved one, navy deployment, and herbal screw ups can all make contributions to the improvement of PTSD in children.

It's crucial to do not forget that no longer anybody who studies a disturbing event will increase PTSD. Factors alongside facet man or woman resilience, coping strategies, genetics, and social assist structures can all play a role in figuring out whether or not or no longer or no longer or no longer PTSD signs and symptoms will increase. Early intervention and suitable assist can help to improve results for teenagers who have professional a worrying event and may be susceptible to growing PTSD.

Common Traumatic Experiences Affecting Teen

Adolescence is a period of vulnerability and transformation, making teenagers liable to hundreds of disturbing critiques that would have prolonged-term outcomes on their intellectual and emotional health. Common demanding stories that teens also can moreover face include physical or sexual abuse, bullying and cyberbullying, community violence, home violence, injuries and injuries, natural disasters, the dearth of a cherished one, medical trauma, sexual attack, battle and warfare, forget and abandonment, and cultural and identification trauma. It is important to do not forget that everyone responds to worrying events in some other manner; a few teenagers also can increase PTSD or different mental health troubles, on the same time as others may moreover display resilience and coping abilities. To assist teens cope with and heal from those worrying activities, it's miles important to offer a secure and supportive environment, similarly to early intervention and professional help.

RECOGNIZING TRIGGERS

Identifying Triggers And Stressors Specific To Teens

Parents, caregivers, educators, and highbrow fitness experts need to have a notable know-how of the developmental stage, social surroundings, and private critiques of young adults to understand their triggers and stressors. Common triggers and stressors that could have an effect on teenagers encompass educational pressure, social media, peer relationships, circle of relatives conflict, body image and appearance, relationships and romantic pursuits, identification exploration, demanding activities, college surroundings, transition intervals, peer rejection, substance abuse and peer stress, parental expectations, destiny uncertainty, media, and statistics. When teenagers can express their feelings and issues in a solid place, adults can help them growth coping techniques and provide steering to assist them manage those tough moments.

Common Traumatic Experiences Affecting Teens

It's crucial to be touchy whilst handling demanding memories that might have an effect on young adults. Here are a number of the most common ones: physical or sexual abuse, bullying and cyberbullying, network violence, home violence, accidents and injuries, herbal disasters, loss of a cherished one, scientific trauma, sexual attack, war and battle, forget and abandonment, cultural and identification trauma, substance abuse, acculturation stress, and parental divorce.

It's essential to provide the proper help to help teenagers cope and heal from the results of trauma. Early intervention, communique, and get right of get admission to to to highbrow health property are important for selling resilience and healing in teenagers who've lengthy long past thru stressful events.

COPING MECHANISMS

Healthy Vs. Unhealthy Coping Strategies

Healthy coping strategies are beneficial and effective techniques for human beings to control stress, feelings, and problems. On the opposite hand, horrible coping techniques may moreover provide quick remedy but should have horrible effects in the end. Here's a assessment amongst wholesome and bad coping techniques:

Healthy Coping Strategies:

Talking and Expressing Feelings: Sharing your emotions with humans you be given as genuine with, like circle of relatives or buddies, or a therapist can help reduce emotional misery and offer guide.

Mindfulness and Meditation: Practicing mindfulness and meditation can assist loosen up you, reduce strain, and enhance emotional well-being.

Physical Activity: Doing everyday workout can launch endorphins, which could enhance your mood and decrease pressure.

Healthy Hobbies: Doing innovative or a laugh sports activities like portray, writing, gambling song, or cooking can be a pleasant way to specific your emotions.

Deep Breathing: Deep respiratory sports activities can help regulate feelings and reduce tension.

Seeking Professional Help: Consult a therapist or counselor for steering and manual whilst managing annoying situations or trauma.

Positive Self-Talk: Using affirmations and effective self-communicate to project terrible thoughts and beautify conceitedness.

Healthy Nutrition and Sleep: Eating balanced food and getting enough sleep can make contributions to ordinary nicely-being and stress discount.

Time Management: Organizing responsibilities and putting priorities can help lessen stress and decorate time management capabilities.

Social Support: Connecting with pals, own family, or manual agencies can provide you with a experience of belonging and emotional consolation.

Unhealthy Coping Strategies:

Substance Abuse: Using alcohol, capsules, or different substances to numb feelings and escape fact.

Avoidance: Ignoring or preserving off troubles in region of addressing them right away.

Isolation: Avoiding social interactions and keeping apart your self from guide networks.

Self-Harm: Doing self-detrimental behaviors like reducing or self-inflicted harm to cope with emotional ache.

Emotional Eating: Eating an excessive amount of or ingesting awful components as a response to stress or feelings.

Risky Behaviour: Doing risky sports activities sports or behaviors that offer brief treatment however have bad effects.

Aggression: Expressing frustration or anger thru competitive behaviors in desire to healthful verbal exchange.

Denial: Refusing to renowned or get maintain of hard feelings or demanding situations.

Excessive Technology Use: Escaping into technology or video display units to avoid managing actual-existence troubles.

Suppression: Pushing away or suppressing emotions without addressing them.

Encouraging and selling healthful coping techniques can help people, which consist of teens, growth powerful strategies to govern strain, assemble resilience, and navigate life's annoying conditions without a doubt and constructively.

Chapter 11: Professional Intervention

Importance of Seeking Help from Mental Health Professionals

Getting help from intellectual fitness professionals is of maximum significance for individuals who are handling emotional, highbrow, or behavioral troubles, which includes PTSD. Here's why it is so critical to are looking for help from intellectual health professionals:

Expertise and Specialized Knowledge: Mental fitness specialists, which includes therapists, counselors, and psychiatrists, have specialized education and facts in understanding and treating a whole lot of intellectual fitness conditions, which encompass PTSD. They have the skills and apprehend-the manner to offer effective interventions and beneficial resource.

Accurate Diagnosis: Mental fitness specialists can successfully observe and diagnose the right mental health situation a person is going via. An correct analysis is vital for developing a custom designed remedy plan that meets the man or woman's unique wishes.

Evidence-Based Treatment: Mental fitness experts are nicely-versed in evidence-primarily based absolutely healing procedures that have been confirmed to be powerful in treating conditions like PTSD. These remedies are subsidized with the useful resource of research and clinical enjoy, developing the chances of quality effects.

Safe and Confidential Environment: Mental health specialists offer a secure, non-public, and nonjudgmental area for humans to speak about their thoughts, emotions, and research. This surroundings encourages open verbal exchange and lets in humans to discover their emotions without fear of stigma or discrimination.

Effective Coping Strategies: Mental health experts can teach individuals wholesome coping strategies and talents to manipulate signs and symptoms and signs, modify emotions, and increase resilience. These techniques offer people the gear to better control disturbing situations.

Medication Management: Psychiatrists and extraordinary clinical experts specializing in intellectual health can prescribe and display screen medication at the same time as vital. Medication can play a top notch position in handling symptoms and enhancing fashionable well-being.

Support and Validation: Mental health professionals provide validation, empathy, and useful resource, supporting people sense understood and much less on my own of their struggles. This emotional help can make a big distinction inside the recuperation way.

Prevention of Escalation: Seeking assist early can prevent the escalation of symptoms and signs and symptoms and the development of extra extreme highbrow fitness troubles. Timely intervention can cause faster recovery and better prolonged-term consequences.

Holistic Approach: Mental fitness specialists take a holistic method to remedy, thinking about different factors together with family dynamics, social help, and way of existence. This entire perspective seems on the individual's well-being from a couple of angles.

Long-Term Well-Being: Working with intellectual fitness professionals can sell lengthy-term intellectual and emotional properly-being. Through ongoing treatment, individuals can take a look at abilties in order to maintain to gain them even after their remedy is over.

In surrender, attempting to find assist from mental health specialists is a proactive step closer to understanding, managing, and overcoming intellectual health stressful conditions. It gives the possibility for growth, healing, and a renewed experience of preference for a brighter destiny.

Types Of Therapy Suitable For Teen Ptsd Treatment

Several types of treatment may be effective in treating PTSD (Post-Traumatic Stress Disorder) in teens. The choice of treatment relies upon at the person's dreams, alternatives, and the severity in their symptoms and symptoms. Here are some kinds of treatment which can be appropriate for teen PTSD remedy:

Cognitive-Behavioral Therapy (CBT): CBT is a broadly used remedy that lets in individuals discover and alternate terrible belief styles and behaviors. It focuses on information how mind, emotions, and behaviors are interconnected. For teens with PTSD, CBT can help them assignment distorted beliefs approximately the demanding occasion, manage distressing emotions, and expand wholesome coping strategies.

Trauma-Focused Cognitive-Behavioral Therapy (TF-CBT): This specialised shape of CBT is custom designed to address trauma-associated problems. TF-CBT consists of exposure treatment, cognitive restructuring, and relaxation techniques to help young adults approach demanding reminiscences, lessen avoidance behaviors, and control signs and symptoms and symptoms and signs.

Eye Movement Desensitization and Reprocessing (EMDR): EMDR is a therapeutic technique that includes guided eye moves or distinct types of bilateral stimulation. It objectives to help people system stressful reminiscences and decrease their emotional effect. EMDR can be mainly effective for teenagers who've professional specific demanding events.

Narrative Exposure Therapy (NET): NET is a structured treatment designed to help human beings, which include young adults, system and integrate worrying reminiscences. It includes developing a narrative of the worrying revel in and the man or woman's existence tale, assisting them gain a sense of coherence and knowledge.

Mindfulness-Based Therapies: Mindfulness-primarily based definitely strategies, including

Mindfulness-Based Stress Reduction (MBSR) or Mindfulness-Based Cognitive Therapy (MBCT), train teenagers a way to live present, manipulate distressing mind, and modify their feelings. These techniques can help lessen reactivity to triggers and decorate common well-being.

Dialectical Behavior Therapy (DBT): DBT is a whole remedy that combines cognitive-behavioral techniques with mindfulness and recognition strategies. It enables human beings regulate emotions, develop interpersonal capabilities, and control distressing situations.

Art Therapy: Art remedy provides a modern outlet for teens to specific their feelings and testimonies through art work workplace work. This can be in particular beneficial for teens who find it hard to verbalize their emotions.

Group Therapy: Group remedy periods offer a supportive surroundings in which teens can percent their reviews, examine from others, and exercise social skills. Group treatment can provide a enjoy of network and decrease feelings of isolation.

Family Therapy: Involving circle of relatives individuals in remedy can help beautify verbal exchange, deal with own family dynamics, and fortify the guide machine for the teen.

It is vital to collaborate with an authorized intellectual health expert who can have a look at the adolescent's requirements and decide the maximum appropriate type of remedy. Treatment has to consist of a combination of remedies and techniques to extend a customized technique that aids the teenager's recovery from PTSD.

Chapter 12: Family Support

Navigating Family Dynamics and Their Impact on Recovery

Navigating own family dynamics and their effect on recuperation is a essential component of assisting a teenager's recovery adventure, specifically at the same time as coping with PTSD. Here's how family dynamics may have an effect on restoration and some strategies to navigate those dynamics efficaciously:

Impact of Family Dynamics:

Support System: A healthful and supportive own family surroundings can provide a robust foundation for a youngster's healing from PTSD. Conversely, circle of relatives conflicts or loss of aid may additionally moreover keep away from improvement.

Triggers and Reminders: Family interactions, communication styles, or awesome own family individuals would likely accidentally reason annoying reminiscences or terrible feelings, affecting the youngster's nicely-being.

Safety and Trust: Rebuilding a enjoy of safety and believe is crucial for recovery. Positive own family dynamics can make a contribution to the teen's functionality to revel in strong and growth wholesome relationships.

Communication: Open and powerful communication inside the own family can foster statistics, reduce misunderstandings, and create a stable area for the youngster to explicit their wishes.

Strategies for Navigating Family Dynamics:

Education and Awareness: Help family individuals understand PTSD, its signs and symptoms and symptoms and symptoms, and the effect it is able to have on the teen's well-being. Education can lessen stigma and foster empathy.

Open Communication: Encourage own family people to pay attention actively and communicate brazenly with the youngster.

Creating an surroundings in which feelings are proven and respected is critical.

Boundaries: Establish smooth obstacles within the family to recognize the youngster's want for location and privacy. Discuss and agree on boundaries that useful resource the teen's restoration.

Family Therapy: Consider regarding the circle of relatives in treatment intervals. Family remedy can deal with communication troubles, sell understanding, and facilitate restoration inside the own family unit.

Normalize Emotions: Teach circle of relatives members a way to answer to the teen's feelings in a non-judgmental and supportive manner. Normalize the experience of emotional u.S.And downs.

Coping Strategies: Teach the own family about wholesome coping strategies that can benefit the teen and the entire own family, fostering a shared sense of well-being.

Consistency and Routine: Establishing a stable ordinary and regular guide from own family individuals can help lessen tension and offer a enjoy of predictability.

Empowerment: Involve the teenager in alternatives about their treatment and recuperation plan. Empower them to take an lively feature in their recuperation approach.

Self-Care for Caregivers: Encourage own family individuals to take care of their very own highbrow and emotional nicely-being. When caregivers are nicely-supported, they might higher assist the teen's recovery.

Professional Guidance: Seek steerage from intellectual health specialists who focus on family remedy or trauma to deal with complex family dynamics efficaciously.

How Parents And Siblings Can Provide A Safe And Supportive Environment

Parents and siblings have a awesome role in offering a sturdy and supportive environment for a youngster dealing with PTSD. Here are some techniques dad and mom and siblings can contribute to developing such an surroundings:

For Parents:

Do Your Research: Learn about PTSD, its symptoms and symptoms and signs and symptoms, and its effects on young adults. Knowing the state of affairs will help you offer informed help.

Open Communication: Make a putting in which your teen feels comfortable speaking about their emotions, studies, and problems. Be a compassionate and non-judgmental listener.

Normalize Reactions: Let your teenager recognize that their reactions and emotions are ordinary responses to trauma. Reassure them that you are there to help them through the restoration procedure.

Be Patient: Recovery takes time. Be affected person along with your teen's development and setbacks, and don't strain them to "get over" their trauma.

Set Boundaries: Respect your youngster's need for location and privateness, at the identical time as moreover maintaining a enjoy of shape and barriers that make them enjoy secure.

Model Healthy Coping: Show healthful coping techniques and self-take care of your private life. Your moves can function great examples for your youngster.

Encourage Professional Help: Support your teen in searching for therapy or counseling, and be involved in their remedy plan with their consent.

Provide Stability: Maintain a regular and predictable recurring, which could help lessen tension and create a experience of safety.

Create a Safe Home: Make extraordinary the bodily surroundings is safe and free from triggers that might worsen your teenager's signs and symptoms.

For Siblings:

Educate Siblings: Help siblings recognize what PTSD is and its effects. Encourage empathy and compassion.

Be Patient and Understanding: Siblings may moreover need to be affected character with temper adjustments or emotional reactions. Encourage open verbal exchange and expression.

Offer Support: Let your teenager recognize you are there for them and willing to pay attention inside the occasion that they need to talk. Sometimes, truely being a supportive presence is sufficient.

Avoid Judgment: Help siblings apprehend that trauma responses are not options but are natural reactions to tough reviews.

Respect Boundaries: Teach siblings to apprehend their traumatized sibling's need for non-public region and privacy.

Include Them in Positive Activities: Participate in extremely good and thrilling sports as a own family or with a sibling. Fun research can help create positive reminiscences.

Encourage Empathy: Help siblings enlarge empathy with the aid of using discussing how they may experience in comparable conditions and by way of the usage of using emphasizing the importance of supporting each different.

Seek Family Therapy: Consider own family remedy to cope with any dynamics that may be affecting the sibling relationship and circle of relatives interactions.

Remember that help from parents and siblings have to have a massive impact on a teenager's healing adventure. Your expertise, staying power, and willingness to look at and adapt ought to make a huge difference in developing a secure and supportive environment to your teenager with PTSD.

Chapter 13: Building Resilience

Strengthening Emotional Resilience in Teens

Strengthening emotional resilience in young adults is vital for supporting them cope with adversity, manage stress, and navigate demanding situations. Here are a few sensible steps to assist them in developing emotional resilience:

Encourage Healthy Connections: Assist teens in forming and maintaining powerful relationships with pals, circle of relatives, and mentors. Having a robust manual network is fundamental.

Teach Problem-Solving Skills: Guide teens through hassle-fixing techniques. Help them smash down annoying situations into smaller steps, give you solutions, and make knowledgeable selections.

Promote Self-Awareness: Help teenagers apprehend and apprehend their emotions. Encourage them to mirror thru journaling or open conversations about their emotions and opinions.

Develop Coping Strategies: Teach teens some of healthful coping strategies which includes deep respiratory, mindfulness, innovative expression, and physical hobby.

Foster Positive Self-Talk: Help teenagers assignment horrible self-communicate and cultivate a greater wonderful and self-compassionate inner communicate.

Model Resilience: Share memories of approaches you have got overcome stressful conditions and confirmed resilience to your very own lifestyles. This can be inspiring and teach precious classes.

Encourage Flexibility: Teach teens to adjust to change and uncertainty. Stress the importance of being open to exquisite perspectives and solutions.

Cultivate Mindfulness: Introduce mindfulness practices to help teens live gift, control strain, and alter their emotions.

Set Realistic Goals: Guide teenagers in setting plausible goals, emphasizing development over perfection. Celebrate their successes alongside the way.

Promote Self-Care: Teach teens to prioritize self-care sports activities that nourish their physical, emotional, and intellectual well-being.

Acknowledge and Validate Emotions: Create a steady location for teenagers to particular their feelings without judgment. Acknowledge their feelings and assist them learn how to manage excessive feelings.

Encourage Resilient Thinking: Teach teens to reframe traumatic conditions as possibilities for growth and getting to know. Encourage a effective and adaptable mind-set.

Provide Autonomy: Support teens in making picks and fixing troubles on their very non-public. Empower them to take initiative and construct self assurance.

Develop Gratitude: Encourage teens to exercise gratitude by the use of focusing at the splendid elements in their lives. Gratitude can foster a experience of appreciation and well-being.

Seek Professional Help: If a teenager is struggling significantly, don't forget regarding a intellectual health professional to offer steering and resource in building emotional resilience.

By guiding teens through the ones techniques, you could help them bring together the capabilities and thoughts-set they want to face existence's demanding situations with resilience, adaptability, and a revel in of empowerment.

Cultivating Positive Self-esteem And Self-well honestly really worth

Cultivating nice vanity and self-worth is vital for young adults' emotional well-being and ordinary development. Here are practical methods to help young adults assemble a healthful experience of self-esteem and self esteem:

Encourage Self-Reflection: Help teens find out their strengths, pursuits, and values. Encourage them to select out what they excel at and what makes them unique.

Celebrate Achievements: Acknowledge and feature a laugh their accomplishments, whether or no longer or no longer large or small. This reinforces the idea that their efforts are valued and crucial.

Promote Self-Compassion: Teach teens to deal with themselves with the same kindness and facts they offer to others. Encourage self-compassionate self-communicate.

Set Realistic Goals: Assist teens in setting possible dreams that project them without overwhelming them. Successes contribute to a feel of competence.

Encourage Healthy Self-Care: Stress the significance of looking after their physical, emotional, and intellectual nicely-being via sports they experience.

Provide Constructive Feedback: Offer comments that specializes in improvement instead of complaint. Help them see errors as possibilities for boom.

Model Positive Self-Esteem: Demonstrate self-reputation and excellent shallowness for your behavior. Be a role version for wholesome self esteem.

Support Individuality: Embrace and have a laugh their individuality. Encourage them to explicit their real selves with out fear of judgment.

Promote Resilience: Teach young adults to cope with setbacks and traumatic conditions really. Show them that setbacks are transient and may be triumph over.

Encourage Positive Affirmations: Help young adults create and use excellent affirmations to counteract terrible self-communicate and beautify their self assure.

Teach Boundaries: Guide them in placing and respecting non-public obstacles, empowering them to prioritize their nicely-being.

Foster Mindfulness: Introduce mindfulness practices to help teenagers stay gift, control stress, and expand self-recognition.

Offer Unconditional Love: Let them recognize you want and be given them for who they're, regardless of achievements or failures.

Create a Supportive Environment: Foster an environment wherein they experience strong to specific themselves, ask questions, and searching for steerage.

Seek Professional Help: If conceitedness struggles are excessive, take into account associated with a intellectual health expert who makes a speciality of arrogance and self-worth problems.

By presenting steerage, guide, and encouragement, you can assist teenagers make bigger a sturdy feel of self esteem and self-esteem that empowers them to face demanding situations, assemble healthy relationships, and lead great lives.

EDUCATIONAL SETTINGS

Addressing Ptsd Challenges In School

Addressing the problems of PTSD in college necessitates a joint strive among college personnel, dad and mom, highbrow fitness experts, and the scholar. Here are some techniques to assist a scholar with PTSD in a college putting:

Open Communication: Stay in everyday contact with the student's parents or guardians, as well as any intellectual fitness specialists concerned in their treatment.

Creating a Supportive Environment: Establish a secure and supportive classroom surroundings in which the pupil feels snug and understood.

Educating School Staff: Provide training to teachers, counselors, and specific team of workers people about PTSD, its signs and signs and symptoms and signs and symptoms, and the way to useful resource college students who may be experiencing it.

Individualized Education Plan (IEP) or 504 Plan: If essential, artwork with the pupil's parents and college team of workers to develop an IEP or 504 plan that outlines resorts and lets in to address their particular desires.

Sensitivity to Triggers: Be aware about capability triggers in the college environment and paintings to restrict or control them. This might also moreover consist of preserving off first rate subjects or conditions that might purpose misery.

Flexible Scheduling: Offer flexibility in assignments, time limits, or elegance schedules to deal with the student's dreams within the direction of times of heightened strain or triggers.

Safe Spaces: Designate a secure space wherein the scholar can pass inside the event that they need a 2d to loosen up or manipulate their emotions.

Emotional Regulation Techniques: Teach the students coping strategies like deep respiration, grounding sporting events, or mindfulness to help them adjust their emotions.

Clear Expectations: Give smooth instructions and expectancies for assignments and study room conduct. Predictable exercises can help lessen tension.

Buddy System: Pair the scholar with a supportive peer who can provide encouragement and help while desired.

Guidance Counseling: Encourage the scholar to apply the faculty's counseling offerings for delivered assist.

Reduced Exposure to Triggers: If possible, artwork with the pupil to discover and decrease exposure to triggers within the university environment.

Transitions: Provide manual throughout transitions among commands, sports activities, or school years, which can be difficult for college children with PTSD.

Positive Reinforcement: Acknowledge and reward the pupil's efforts and achievements. Positive feedback can enhance their confidence and conceitedness.

Promoting Inclusion: Urge social interactions and possibilities for the student to have interaction with peers, fostering a enjoy of belonging.

Professional Guidance: If critical, contain highbrow fitness specialists who can offer steering, guide, and interventions tailor-made to the student's dreams.

Collaboration and empathy are crucial whilst addressing PTSD problems inside the school setting. By running together, college groups can create an inclusive and supportive surroundings that promotes the student's properly-being and educational success.

Strategies For Teachers And Administrators To Support Affected Teens

Teachers and directors have a primary characteristic in supporting teens with PTSD (Post-Traumatic Stress Disorder) within the school placing. Here are some processes to create a supportive and inclusive surroundings:

For Teachers:

Educate Yourself: Get to understand approximately PTSD, its signs, and the manner it influences students' studying and conduct. This expertise will guide your interactions and manual.

Open Communication: Keep open communication with the pupil, their parents or caregivers, and any intellectual health specialists worried.

Provide a Safe Space: Make a look at room surroundings in which the pupil feels physical and emotionally safe. This can consist of having a chosen strong location in the lecture room.

Accommodate Triggers: Be aware of functionality triggers and artwork to lessen exposure. Allow the scholar to step out or take breaks if wanted.

Flexible Assignments: Offer flexibility with assignments, cut-off dates, or checks subsequently of times of accelerated pressure or triggers.

Provide Clear Instructions: Give clean and concise commands for assignments and have a look at room sports. Predictable workouts can help lessen anxiety.

Emotional Regulation Techniques: Teach and encourage the use of coping strategies like deep breathing, mindfulness, or guided imagery to assist the student control their feelings.

Peer Support: Match the student with a supportive peer who can offer help, friendship, and encouragement.

Positive Reinforcement: Acknowledge and praise the student's efforts and achievements. Positive feedback can decorate their vanity.

Empathy and Understanding: Show empathy and records in the direction of the pupil's disturbing conditions. Validate their emotions and research.

For Administrators:

Training: Provide expert improvement for instructors and team of workers on PTSD attention, sensitivity, and powerful help techniques.

Collaboration: Foster collaboration among instructors, counselors, and one-of-a-type help group of workers to make certain a whole technique to the scholar's well-being.

Chapter 14: Peer Relationships

Encouraging Healthy Friendships and Connections

Teens' social and emotional improvement wants to foster healthy friendships and connections. Positive relationships can provide guide, promote well-being, and create a experience of belonging. Here are some pointers to assist young adults construct and maintain healthful relationships:

Model excellent conduct in your relationships to expose teenagers the way to talk, empathize, and respect others.

Teach teenagers effective conversation, lively listening, conflict decision, and empathy.

Encourage inclusivity and recognition of variations.

Organize enterprise sports or tasks that promote collaboration and teamwork.

Set up peer mentorship or help programs for older young adults to assist more youthful college college college students.

Train teens to specific their desires and obstacles assertively at the same time as respecting the ones of others.

Discuss the importance of respectful and steady online interactions.

Plan social sports together with game nights, film nights, or community provider projects.

Help teens attention on constructing some close, significant friendships.

Teach teenagers a manner to navigate conflicts constructively.

Train teens to be wonderful listeners and offer emotional manual to their pals.

Discuss the significance of influencing friends in high-quality strategies.

Normalize vulnerability and inspire teens to percentage their emotions with relied on buddies.

Suggest undertaking shared pursuits, sports activities activities sports, or interests.

Educate teens about recognizing and distancing themselves from poisonous relationships.

Encourage teens to reap out to depended on adults for advice or useful resource.

By fostering wholesome friendships and connections, teens can gain from emotional boom, resilience, and regular happiness. Providing guidance and growing a supportive surroundings can help them boom substantial and lasting relationships that actually impact their lives.

Fostering A Sense Of Belonging Among Peers

Creating a supportive and inclusive social surroundings for young adults is essential, and fostering a experience of belonging among pals is high. Here are a few thoughts for selling a sturdy experience of belonging:

Organize sports that cater to incredible interests and skills, so everybody can participate and make a contribution. Plan team-constructing video video games or sports that inspire collaboration and assist teenagers bond. Set up tasks or projects that require teamwork and cooperation, giving young adults a not unusual aim. Establish mentorship or friend systems in which older teenagers manual and help extra youthful friends. Form clubs or corporations based totally mostly on shared interests, pastimes, or research, so teens with commonalities can join. Organize volunteer opportunities that permit teenagers to work together for a considerable motive, fostering a revel in of group spirit and reason. Encourage open and respectful discussions about variety, inclusion, and popularity. Highlight and have fun the perfect abilties and backgrounds of every person, selling an surroundings in which range is valued. Empower young adults to take the lead in organizing sports or campaigns that promote inclusivity and belonging. Recognize and reward powerful conduct, acts of kindness, and efforts to create an inclusive surroundings. Teach young adults powerful war choice techniques that emphasize understanding, empathy, and locating common ground. Implement anti-bullying applications and discussions to create a secure and respectful social environment. Foster empathy by encouraging young adults to position themselves in each unique's shoes and understand every other's critiques. Pair young adults with mentors who can provide guidance, manual, and a experience of belonging. Encourage young adults to advantage out to beginners and motive them to experience welcome in the social circle. Create possibilities for smaller, intimate gatherings in which teens should have giant conversations and build deeper connections. Express gratitude for everyone's contributions and presence in the employer. Highlight excessive excellent characteristic fashions who exemplify the values of inclusivity, empathy, and popularity.

By the use of the ones techniques, you can create an surroundings wherein all teenagers revel in valued, vast, and empowered to be their actual selves.

HOLISTIC WELL-BEING

Incorporating Physical Health And Exercise In Recovery

Incorporating physical fitness and exercising into the recuperation gadget may be fairly beneficial for people, together with teenagers, who're dealing with issues along with PTSD. Physical interest may want to have a first rate impact on intellectual fitness, lessen stress, and make a contribution to essential nicely-being. Here are a few tips at the way to integrate bodily health and exercise into the recovery adventure:

1. Speak to a Healthcare Professional: Before beginning any workout software program application, especially for human beings with

clinical or intellectual conditions, it's critical to are seeking for recommendation from a healthcare expert or intellectual fitness provider to make certain the chosen sports are steady and appropriate.

2. Mindful Movement: Engage in conscious physical sports activities along aspect yoga, tai chi, or qigong. These practices combine motion with deep respiratory and meditation, that may help to loosen up and decrease strain.

three. Aerobic Exercise: Activities like brisk on foot, taking walks, cycling, or swimming can assist elevate your temper, reduce anxiety, and decorate cardiovascular fitness.

four. Strength Training: Incorporate energy schooling bodily activities using body weight, resistance bands, or weights. Building strength can assist to beautify self-self assurance and frame picture.

5. Team Sports: Participate in crew sports activities or agency fitness training to foster a

experience of camaraderie and social connection.

6. Nature Walks: Spend time exterior in nature, whether or not it's far taking walks in a park, trekking a course, or truely taking part inside the easy air. Nature may additionally need to have a calming and rejuvenating effect.

7. Dance: Dancing is a amusing and expressive way to enhance temper, enhance frame interest, and release stress.

eight. Set Realistic Goals: Establish possible fitness dreams and track improvement through the years. This revel in of fulfillment can help to increase arrogance and motivation.

nine. Consistency: Incorporate ordinary bodily interest proper into a every day or weekly habitual. Consistency is essential for reaping the prolonged-time period advantages of exercise.

10. Mind-Body Connection: Encourage young adults to track into their bodies and turn out to be aware of how workout makes them experience physical and emotionally.

11. Mindfulness During Exercise: Practice mindfulness even as exercise, focusing on the sensations of motion, breathing, and the prevailing 2nd.

12. Creative Activities: Engage in sports activities like dance, martial arts, or mountain climbing that provide each physical motion and modern expression.

thirteen. Adaptive Activities: Choose sports activities that align with individual opportunities and physical skills, making sure a notable and exciting enjoy.

14. Social Engagement: Invite buddies or family humans to enroll in in physical sports activities, promoting social interaction and assist.

15. Progressive Relaxation: Incorporate relaxation strategies, which include stretching

or modern muscle relaxation, after physical interest to further lessen tension.

It's vital to find out amusing and sustainable kinds of physical interest that make contributions to properly-being. Encouraging a balanced technique to bodily health, in mixture with highbrow health help, can help to beautify the restoration way and reason an regular sense of empowerment and resilience.

Mindfulness, Meditation, And Relaxation Techniques For Teens

Mindfulness, meditation, and relaxation strategies may be extensively beneficial for teens, supporting them control pressure, improve recognition, and enhance number one properly-being. Here are a few techniques which can be properly-ideal for teens:

Chapter 15: Digital Age Challenges

Navigating Social Media Triggers and Online Stressors

Teens need to learn how to manage the traumatic conditions of social media and on-line interactions in current-day virtual age. Here are some strategies to assist them accomplish that:

Take a Digital Detox: Suggest normal breaks from social media to reduce exposure to triggers and on-line stressors. Designate tech-unfastened times or days.

Be Mindful of What You Consume: Teach teenagers to be aware about the content fabric cloth they consume online. Suggest they unfollow or mute accounts that motive terrible emotions.

Understand Filters: Discuss how social media regularly gives a filtered and curated version of fact, helping young adults apprehend that what they see isn't the whole picture.

Set Boundaries: Help teenagers set up healthy boundaries for social media use, collectively with time limits and exclusive "no-cellphone" zones.

Be Kind Online: Teach teenagers to engage in powerful and empathetic on line interactions. Urge them to be type, respectful, and considerate in their online communications.

Be Selective About What You Share: Advise young adults to bear in thoughts of what they percentage online. Remind them that they have control over their digital footprint.

Unplug Before Bed: Encourage young adults to disconnect from video show gadgets as a minimum an hour earlier than bedtime to sell higher sleep high-quality.

Recognize Triggers: Help teenagers grow to be aware of specific content fabric material or conditions that motive terrible emotions. Urge them to be careful about engaging with such content material fabric.

Prioritize Real-Life Connections: Encourage young adults to prioritize face-to-face interactions and offline sports activities over virtual interactions.

Learn Digital Citizenship: Promote discussions approximately responsible and moral online conduct, together with a way to cope with cyberbullying and resource peers.

Explore Offline Interests: Encourage teens to discover pastimes and interests outdoor of social media, helping them discover success beyond the virtual global.

Think Critically: Teach teenagers to significantly evaluate information they come upon online, in conjunction with truth-checking and verifying property.

Use Positive Affirmations: Encourage young adults to use great affirmations to counteract terrible thoughts or comparisons added on thru social media.

Report and Block: Instruct young adults on the way to document and block beside the point or risky content material, further to human beings carrying out cyberbullying.

Seek Support: Emphasize the importance of in search of beneficial aid from depended on pals, own family members, or highbrow health professionals if on line stressors emerge as overwhelming.

Be a Good Role Model: Model healthy social media habits and show them a way to control triggers and stressors certainly.

By training teens to navigate social media mindfully and growth resilience in the direction of on-line stressors, you may help them use generation in approaches that beautify their well-being and intellectual health. Open verbal exchange and ongoing steerage are key in assisting teenagers boom a healthful dating with the virtual worldwide.

Balancing Technology Use For Mental Well-being

Balancing era use for intellectual properly-being is critical in cutting-edge-day virtual age. Here are sensible guidelines to assist young adults hold a healthy dating with era whilst prioritizing their intellectual health:

Set Boundaries: Establish easy boundaries for display time, every in phrases of length and specific instances of day. Create a balance amongst on line and offline sports activities.

Tech-Free Zones: Designate remarkable regions, together with bedrooms or mealtime regions, as tech-unfastened zones to promote relaxation and connection.

Mindful Consumption: Encourage young adults to apprehend of the content they consume online. Help them recognize at the identical time as certain content cloth negatively impacts their temper or nicely-being.

Scheduled Breaks: Incorporate ordinary breaks from monitors in the course of take a look at or leisure time. Use breaks for bodily activity, relaxation, or face-to-face interactions.

Digital Detox: Plan occasional virtual detox periods, which include weekends or vacations, wherein young adults disconnect from shows and consciousness on offline sports activities.

Prioritize Sleep: Emphasize the significance of brilliant sleep with the aid of encouraging teenagers to disconnect from video display gadgets at least an hour in advance than bedtime.

Mindful Notifications: Teach teenagers to control notifications and prioritize vital messages, decreasing normal distractions and capability stressors.

Engage in Real-Life Activities: Encourage teens to pursue hobbies, sports activities sports, and innovative activities that provide a revel in of feat and entertainment offline.

Social Interaction: Promote face-to-face interactions with friends and family to foster actual connections and assist social well-being.

Digital Well-being Tools: Utilize included virtual well-being capabilities on devices to music show time and set usage limits.

Practice Mindfulness: Introduce mindfulness strategies to assist teenagers stay present and manipulate pressure, even even as the use of technology.

Model Healthy Behavior: Demonstrate balanced era use and mindfulness on your very own lifestyles, serving as a incredible function version.

Educate About Impact: Help teenagers understand how excessive technology use can impact intellectual fitness, sleep, and common well-being.

Chapter 16: Reshaping the Narrative

Challenging Negative Beliefs and Thoughts

Helping teens project their horrible beliefs and mind is a key functionality that would have a large effect on their intellectual and emotional fitness. Here's a step-through way of-step approach to assist them reframe their horrible wondering:

1. Recognize Negative Thoughts: Encourage young adults to end up privy to their horrific thoughts and beliefs. Help them discover at the same time as those mind upward thrust up and the manner they've an impact on their emotions.

2. Analyze the Evidence: Ask them to take a look at the proof that enables their terrible notion. Is there concrete evidence for their concept, or is it primarily based on assumptions or perceptions?

3. Consider Other Perspectives: Guide teens to consider different viable factors for the

situation. Are there excellent views that would offer a more balanced view?

four. Evaluate the Situation: Encourage them to evaluate whether or not their terrible notion is an exaggeration or a totally bad interpretation of the scenario.

five. Challenge Cognitive Distortions: Teach teenagers about not unusual cognitive distortions, which incorporates black-and-white wondering, catastrophizing, and personalization. Help them pick out and assignment those distortions.

6. Generate Positive Thoughts: Have them generate counterarguments or opportunity thoughts that mission the awful notion. What are more balanced and rational methods of considering the scenario?

7. Practice Self-Compassion: Teach young adults to cope with themselves with self-compassion. Help them reframe bad self-talk with type and supportive language.

eight. Focus on Strengths and Achievements: Encourage them to shift their interest to their strengths, accomplishments, and incredible capabilities. This can help counter feelings of inadequacy.

9. Use Mindfulness Techniques: Introduce mindfulness practices to help young adults take a look at their mind with out judgment and permit cross of rumination.

10. Challenge Core Beliefs: If terrible mind stem from deep-seated middle beliefs, artwork with them to mission and reevaluate the ones ideals through the years.

eleven. Visualize Success: Guide teens to visualise themselves efficiently overcoming traumatic conditions and attaining their dreams. Visualization can sell a greater incredible thoughts-set.

12. Journaling: Suggest keeping a journal to document terrible mind after which find out alternative, greater awesome views.

thirteen. Encourage Problem-Solving: Shift the point of interest from residing on troubles to brainstorming practical answers and actionable steps.

14. Seek Support: Teach young adults to reach out to friends, circle of relatives individuals, or intellectual health experts for help and attitude.

15. Practice Gratitude: Cultivate a addiction of specializing in high exceptional elements of existence through gratitude sporting events. This can assist shift their interest faraway from negativity.

16. Celebrate Progress: Acknowledge and characteristic amusing even small victories in tough bad beliefs and thoughts.

By guiding young adults via the ones steps, you could assist them boom a extra healthy attitude and build resilience in the direction of lousy thinking patterns. With consistent exercising, they can domesticate a extra awesome and balanced outlook on themselves and their reviews.

Promoting A Sense Of Agency And Control In Teen

Fostering a experience of autonomy and control in teenagers is essential for their personal increase, self-self notion, and average properly-being. Here are a few techniques to help them extend a robust enjoy of organisation and manipulate:

Encourage Decision-Making: Give teenagers the chance to make alternatives, each at domestic and of their activities, and permit them to have a examine from the effects.

Set Realistic Goals: Help teenagers set capacity goals that they may artwork inside the course of. Break down large desires into smaller, more feasible steps.

Problem-Solving Skills: Teach teenagers hassle-solving techniques and inspire them to find out solutions to any issues they come upon.

Autonomy and Responsibility: Give teenagers age-suitable responsibilities that make contributions to the household or community. This will assist them experience accountable and satisfied with their accomplishments.

Encourage Self-Expression: Create an surroundings wherein young adults experience snug expressing their critiques, mind, and emotions without worry of judgment.

Supportive Guidance: Offer steerage and recommendation whilst desired, however additionally permit teens take the lead in finding their solutions.

Celebrate Independence: Acknowledge and feature fun moments at the identical time as teens take initiative and display independence.

Encourage Skill-Building: Help teens increase new competencies or pursue pursuits they'll be obsessed with. This will offer them the energy to take fee of their increase.

Model Empowerment: Show teens how you address demanding situations, setbacks, and choice-making in a assured and empowered way.

Positive Self-Talk: Teach teenagers to use wonderful self-speak and affirmations to enhance their revel in of business enterprise and self-efficacy.

Teach Assertiveness: Guide teenagers in talking their needs, barriers, and choices assertively and respectfully.

Time Management: Help teenagers increase effective time control abilties, permitting them to prioritize duties and obligations.

Embrace Failure as Learning: Encourage teenagers to view disasters as reading opportunities in area of as setbacks.

Reflect and Learn: Have ordinary conversations with teens about their critiques, successes, and regions for development.

Encourage Advocacy: Teach teenagers to indicate for themselves, whether or not it's far in school, extracurricular activities, or social situations.

Healthy Risk-Taking: Support calculated dangers that allow teenagers step outside their consolation zones and bring together resilience.

Mindfulness Practice: Introduce mindfulness practices that help teens stay present and make conscious choices.

Provide a Safety Net: Let teenagers comprehend which you're there to provide assist and steering in the event that they ever need it, giving them a experience of protection as they make alternatives.

By fostering a revel in of organization and manage, you can provide teenagers the self notion, talents, and attitude they need to stand traumatic conditions and take gain of possibilities in their lives.

Chapter 17: Success Stories

Inspiring Accounts of Teens Who Triumphed Over Ptsd

Absolutely! Here are a few extraordinary tales of teenagers who have overcome PTSD:

Alex's Journey to Recovery: Alex, a teenager who professional a demanding event, had to cope with PTSD for a long term. With the help of remedy, guide companies, and their family's unwavering aid, Alex have end up capable of gradually triumph over their signs. With energy of thoughts and resilience, they grew to end up their enjoy right into a platform to raise hobby about intellectual fitness and help others on their healing journeys.

Samantha's Resilience: After surviving a essential twist of future, Samantha had to war immoderate PTSD that disrupted her life and relationships. With the help of remedy and mindfulness practices, she found out coping techniques to govern her signs and symptoms and symptoms. Samantha ultimately used her critiques to jot down and create artwork, which now not best aided her healing but additionally inspired many others managing similar disturbing conditions.

Jake's Road to Empowerment: Jake, a teenager who faced youngsters trauma, had to cope with PTSD and its effects on his shallowness and social interactions. Through remedy, he received insights into his triggers and located strategies to regain control over his emotions. Jake's adventure led him to become an propose for intellectual health interest in schools, sharing his tale and inspiring open conversations approximately highbrow nicely-being.

Emily's Path to Empathy: Emily's existence modified substantially after a worrying incident, fundamental to intense PTSD signs and symptoms. With the assist of treatment and the help of her pals and family, Emily started out to rebuild her existence. What made her journey unique have become her preference to volunteer at a community enterprise that lets in survivors of trauma. By connecting with others who shared comparable reports, Emily placed a deeper cause and revel in of empathy, which performed a important feature in her recovery way.

Aiden's Triumph Through Creativity: Aiden, a teenager who skilled a stressful event, had to cope with nightmares and tension because of PTSD. However, his ardour for music have become a powerful device for healing. Aiden channeled his feelings into songwriting and playing devices, allowing him to express his feelings healthily. His track no longer most effective aided his recovery however moreover stimulated others who decided solace in his lyrics and melodies.

Lila's Journey of Self-Discovery: Lila's battle with PTSD started out out after a series of tough reports. Over time, she explored particular healing tactics, from art work remedy to meditation. Through those explorations, Lila decided her internal power and resilience. She embraced a holistic approach to healing, incorporating bodily sports, progressive pastimes, and self-care rituals into her each day routine. Lila's story serves as a reminder that healing is a multi-faceted journey that entails nurturing all components of oneself.

These tremendous reminiscences show the electricity, dedication, and resilience of teenagers who faced PTSD and emerged more potent. Their journeys are a testomony to the energy of trying to find help, finding healthful coping mechanisms, and the usage of their opinions to encourage and beneficial resource others.

Motivating Others Through Real-existence Recovery Journeys

Motivating others via manner of sharing real-life recuperation tales can be a exquisite deliver of need and idea for those coping with stressful conditions. Here are some key factors to bear in mind at the same time as sharing the ones stories to encourage and uplift others:

Authenticity: It's critical to be actual and honest whilst sharing recollections, highlighting both the struggles and the successes. This lets in create a relatable and sincere connection with the aim marketplace.

Resilience: Showcase the resilience and power that individuals have set up sooner or later in their healing adventure. Highlight moments of perseverance, strength of will, and overcoming barriers.

Positive Transformation: Illustrate the top notch modifications and boom that passed off because of the healing manner. Show how stressful conditions have been changed into opportunities for private development.

Coping Strategies: Discuss the coping techniques, techniques, and device that were instrumental in navigating the recovery journey. Provide sensible insights that others can study to their situations.

Support Network: Highlight the significance of a strong resource network, whether or now not or not it's far own family, friends, mentors, or highbrow fitness experts. Showcase how the ones relationships contributed to the character's development.

Turning Setbacks into Comebacks: Share times wherein setbacks or relapses occurred, but the person persevered and in the long run completed their dreams. This reinforces the concept that setbacks are a part of the journey and may motive even extra comebacks.

Hope and Inspiration: Convey a experience of choice and optimism at some point of the narrative. Inspire others by means of demonstrating that recovery is feasible, even within the face of adversity.

Personal Insights: Offer non-public insights and reflections on the recuperation journey. Discuss schooling determined, self-discoveries, and shifts in perspective that contributed to recuperation.

Visual and Emotional Impact: Incorporate visuals, consisting of pics or movies, to decorate the emotional effect of the story. Visual factors can help the audience connect on a deeper degree.

Empathy and Relatability: Share relatable moments and feelings that others may additionally have skilled. When the target market can empathize with the demanding situations confronted, they may be much more likely to find out motivation within the tale.

Encouraging Action: End the tale with the useful resource of encouraging the target audience to take immoderate fine steps in the path in their private recovery or non-public increase. Provide assets or suggestions for looking for assist and making adjustments.

Ongoing Journey: Stress that recuperation is an ongoing gadget, and it is okay to are looking for assist and preserve working on nicely-being through the years.

Diverse Perspectives: Highlight masses of healing journeys from first-rate backgrounds, evaluations, and stressful situations to reveal off the universality of the human enjoy.

Sharing those reminiscences via numerous systems, which include social media, blogs, motion pics, or public speakme engagements, may be a effective deliver of motivation and encouragement for those on their paths to restoration.

Chapter 18: Long-Term Strategies

Creating a Sustainable Plan For Maintaining Progress

Creating a plan for preserving development is crucial for ensuring that excessive great modifications and boom hold over the lengthy haul. Whether it's miles related to highbrow health, non-public improvement, or each different location of lifestyles, here is a step-with the aid of-step manual to developing a sustainable plan:

Reflect on Your Goals: Start with the resource of clarifying your dreams and the development you've got got already made. Think approximately what you have found and completed thus far.

Identify Key Factors: Figure out the key elements which have contributed for your improvement. These might be particular strategies, carrying activities, behavior, or help systems.

Set Realistic Expectations: Set practical and potential expectancies for the long time. Remember that retaining improvement is a sluggish machine with highs and lows.

Develop Consistent Habits: Focus on forming consistent behavior that useful resource your goals. Identify the actions you can address a every day or weekly foundation to preserve your improvement going.

Create a Routine: Structure your days and weeks with a normal that includes the behavior and sports that have been useful for you.

Monitor and Track: Monitor your actions, mind, and emotions to maintain track of your development. Use journals, apps, or one of a kind device to music your adventure.

Anticipate Challenges: Identify ability traumatic conditions or boundaries which can stand up and give you strategies to overcome them. Having a plan in region will assist you stay resilient.

Adaptability: Recognize that existence is dynamic, and times can also furthermore change. Be organized to regulate your plan as needed to accommodate new traumatic conditions or possibilities.

Self-Care and Balance: Make self-care a mission and maintain a healthy paintings-lifestyles stability. Allocate time for relaxation, entertainment sports activities sports, and self-mirrored photo.

Seek Support: Keep searching out assist from buddies, own family, mentors, or experts as preferred. A strong help community can provide steerage and encouragement.

Celebrate Achievements: Acknowledge and feature a great time milestones along the manner. Celebrating your achievements reinforces your motivation to preserve going.

Review and Adjust: Regularly evaluation your progress and decide whether or not or not or no longer your plan stays powerful. Make changes based totally mostly on what you've found out.

Long-Term Goals: Keep your prolonged-term goals in mind at the equal time as focusing on the smaller steps you're taking each day. This permits preserve attitude and motivation.

Mindfulness and Reflection: Practice mindfulness and self-reflection to stay in track together along with your desires, feelings, and improvement.

Continued Learning: Stay curious and open to continued learning and private boom. Explore new techniques and insights that align together together with your goals.

Celebrate Small Wins: Celebrate even the small achievements and wonderful moments. Each breakthrough contributes in your common development.

Stay Positive: Cultivate a effective thoughts-set and workout self-compassion. Embrace setbacks as possibilities for learning and growth.

Share Your Journey: Consider sharing your development and evaluations with others. Not fine does this inspire them, however it additionally reinforces your dedication on your dreams.

Remember that retaining improvement is a journey, and it's miles true sufficient to have setbacks alongside the way. The key is to keep studying, adapting, and persevering as you discern within the course of your goals and maintain your direction of growth and improvement.

Preparing Teens For Potential Future Triggers

Helping young adults prepare for capacity triggers within the future consists of equipping them with the equipment, information, and strategies to efficiently control and address tough conditions. Here are some procedures to help teens in searching in advance to and navigating capability triggers:

Educate and Raise Awareness: Teach teenagers approximately common triggers related to their research or instances. Help them apprehend how triggers may want to have an impact on their feelings and reactions.

Open Dialogue: Create an surroundings wherein young adults enjoy comfortable discussing their issues and fears. Encourage them to share any beyond triggers they have got recognized.

Recognize Personal Triggers: Work together to pick out potential triggers that might get up in their each day lives, social interactions, or specific environments.

Teach teens quite a few coping strategies, together with deep respiration, mindfulness, grounding strategies, and outstanding self-speak.

Self-Care Plan: Help teens create a personalized self-care plan that consists of sports and practices they are able to turn to whilst going via triggers.

Support System: Urge teens to pick out depended on friends, circle of relatives people, or mentors they may achieve out to for help while triggers stand up.

Distraction Techniques: Provide techniques for redirecting interest faraway from triggers, such as wearing out a hobby, analyzing, or taking note of song.

Resilience Building: Teach young adults the way to assemble resilience thru that specialize in their strengths, fostering a growth mind-set, and gaining knowledge of from worrying situations.

Role-Playing: Practice situations wherein triggers would possibly upward push up and function-play appropriate responses and coping strategies.

Emergency Action Plan: Develop a plan for excessive triggers or conditions that would require immediately intervention, together with contacting a highbrow fitness professional.

Positive Affirmations: Help teens create and use fantastic affirmations that they may repeat to themselves whilst dealing with triggers.

Goal Setting: Set precise dreams associated with coping with triggers and offer ongoing encouragement and reinforcement.

Stress Reduction Techniques: Teach teens pressure-bargain techniques like workout, journaling, contemporary muscle rest, or conducting innovative sports activities.

Mindful Exposure: Gradually divulge young adults to triggers in a managed and supportive surroundings to assist them assemble tolerance and decrease reactivity.

Distancing Techniques: Teach young adults to mentally "step once more" from triggering situations and feature a have a look at them objectively, that could help reduce emotional intensity.

Responsible Technology Use: Guide teens within the utilization of era mindfully and safely to avoid on line triggers or terrible content material.

Professional Support: Stress the importance of searching out professional assist if triggers are inflicting huge misery or impairment.

Self-Reflection: Encourage young adults to mirror on their studies and have a look at from them, identifying effective strategies for dealing with triggers.

By equipping young adults with these strategies and competencies, they could method capability triggers with resilience, self notion, and a enjoy of manipulate. By getting prepared them to face traumatic situations head-on, you assist them construct precious lifestyles skills as a manner to serve them well in the destiny.

Chapter 19: Advocacy and Awareness
Encouraging Open Dialogue about Teen Ptsd

Talking about youngster PTSD is important for raising popularity, decreasing stigma, and supplying guide. Here are some ways to begin conversations approximately this crucial scenario depends:

Educate Yourself: Learn approximately PTSD in young adults, its reasons, symptoms, and remedies. This will assist you begin conversations.

Create Safe Spaces: Make high-quality young adults revel in snug discussing their thoughts, emotions, and stories without worry of judgment.

Normalize the Conversation: Make highbrow fitness, which includes PTSD, a regular part of circle of relatives or agency conversations.

Share Information: Share correct and relatable information approximately teenager PTSD via articles, movies, books, or professional online sources.

Personal Stories: Share non-public testimonies or critiques associated with highbrow fitness to encourage young adults to speak approximately their struggles.

Use Media and Art: Use films, documentaries, books, or art work to provoke conversations and offer an area to begin for discussing PTSD.

Lead through Example: Talk approximately your emotions and opinions, displaying that it is good enough to speak approximately difficult emotions.

Ask Open-Ended Questions: Ask open-ended questions that invite communique and inspire young adults to proportion their mind.

Listen Actively: Listen patiently and empathetically. Give teenagers the gap to explicit themselves without interruption.

Avoid Judgment: Don't make judgments or provide instant answers. Let young adults recognize that their emotions are legitimate and revered.

www.ingramcontent.com/pod-product-compliance
Lightning Source LLC
Chambersburg PA
CBHW051727020426
42333CB00014B/1199